CHRYSANTHEMUM

Reaktion's Botanical series is the first of its kind, integrating horticultural and botanical writing with a broader account of the cultural and social impact of trees, plants and flowers.

Published
Apple Marcia Reiss
Bamboo Susanne Lucas
Berries Victoria Dickenson
Birch Anna Lewington
Cactus Dan Torre
Cannabis Chris Duvall
Carnation Twigs Way
Carnivorous Plants Dan Torre
Chrysanthemum Twigs Way
Geranium Kasia Boddy
Grasses Stephen A. Harris
Lily Marcia Reiss
Mulberry Peter Coles
Oak Peter Young
Palm Fred Gray
Pine Laura Mason
Poppy Andrew Lack
Primrose Elizabeth Lawson
Rhododendron Richard Milne
Rose Catherine Horwood
Snowdrop Gail Harland
Sunflowers Stephen A. Harris
Tulip Celia Fisher
Weeds Nina Edwards
Willow Alison Syme
Yew Fred Hageneder

CHRYSANTHEMUM

Twigs Way

REAKTION BOOKS

Published by
REAKTION BOOKS LTD
Unit 32, Waterside
44–48 Wharf Road
London N1 7UX, UK

www.reaktionbooks.co.uk

First published 2020

Printed and bound in India by Replika Press Pvt. Ltd

A catalogue record for this book is available from the British Library

ISBN 978 1 78914 205 1

Contents

※

Chrysanthemum 'Ticonderoga'.

Introduction

If you would be happy for a lifetime, grow chrysanthemums.

CHINESE PROVERB

From philosophy to art, ceramics to silks, medicine to death: the chrysanthemum winds its way through ancient Chinese culture to the imperial courts of Japan and onto the canvases and pages of Western civilization. Often dismissed as the 'showman's flower' it draws its allure from the gold of the Sun and the rule of emperors, with sunset shades beloved by East and West. The delicacy of its petals, combined with a long flowering period, gained it the affection of the ancient Chinese, who named it *Chu*, from which comes the name of the ancient city Ta-chu Hsien. Featured on porcelains and silks, the chrysanthemum was prominent in Chinese art as well as being used in traditional medicines. Indeed the 'golden flower' is said to bring health and happiness, long life and a bright future, with a side helping of cheerfulness and sincerity, even before one imbibes it. Coming to Europe with the opening up of Chinese trade in the eighteenth century, the flower was given a new baptism and *chu* or *kiku* became chrysanthemum, named from the Greek for gold (*chrysos*) and for flower (*anthos*). Ironically, it was not until the importation of 'Old Purple', a plum-red variety, that the possibilities of the chrysanthemum were truly appreciated in the West as the cheering yellow colours of the original wild chrysanthemum multiplied into an array of autumnal hues. Filling the autumn months, they

East meets West in William Morris Arts and Crafts chrysanthemum wallpaper, 1876.

give rise to associations varying from remembrance of ancestors to the start of the American football season – the latter an occasion to which it was long a tradition to wear a chrysanthemum buttonhole. In America the tradition of Thanksgiving was soon regarded as incomplete without a bunch of chrysanthemums, despite the fact that they only arrived on the continent in the late eighteenth century.

Beloved by Impressionist painters for its warm tones and exoticism, the chrysanthemum was taken up with enthusiasm across Europe in the late nineteenth century, appearing in the theatre, literature and even academic works as the motif of the East. The complex religious and philosophical attributes of the chrysanthemum did not, however, transfer so easily and so the concept of yang, the celebration of the 'double nine' and the emblem of long life, was lost and the flower literally hovered between life and death as parts of Europe associated it with the graveside. Its appearance in literature, both of the East and West, echoes these contrasts, from the Japanese haiku to the novellas of John Steinbeck, D. H. Lawrence and Saki. The exquisite but scentless flower entered Western literature with mixed messages of sexuality and feminism, but with an ability to take centre stage at numerous flower shows with its mop-heads of colour through the bleakest times of the year. Taken up by public parks and gardens across the USA and UK, chrysanthemums inspired specialist glasshouses entirely devoted to their care and show, and supposedly lowered the numbers of urban suicides with their tints of summer in autumn. Truly a flower that spans the history and art of cultures around the globe.

From literature and art we turn to science. Sadly, for a flower so beneficial to mind and body and so universally beloved, the genus *Chrysanthemum* into which all the garden chrysanthemums belong is now a much reduced one. Recent advances in the phylogenetics of the plant world have reduced the chrysanthemum to a mere thirty familiar species, ousting the likes of feverfew, ox-eye daisies, marguerites and Shasta daisies, which were once proud members of the chrysanthemum fold, and scattering them instead among the

The chrysanthemum petal can be bred to extreme shapes and lengths.

A typical greeting card for the autumn season, with chrysanthemums depicted on the right.

Leucanthemum, Argyranthemum, Glebionis and the *Tanacetum*, from where they are given an honourable mention in our final chapter. For a short while the beloved florists' chrysanthemum was itself removed from the genus and deposited unceremoniously in the genus *Dendranthema*, but thankfully a ruling of the International Botanical Congress in 1999 changed the defining species of the genus to *Chrysanthemum indicum*. This restored the florists' chrysanthemum to the genus *Chrysanthemum* by neatly changing the definition of what constituted a chrysanthemum – a plant type from which most chrysanthemums had, of course, descended. The botanical history of the chrysanthemums is indeed a complex one, made more so by the intense hybridization that has been encouraged over the history of cultivation and a tendency to polyploidy (having more than one set of chromosomes), so that despite the rapidly decreasing number of species, there are literally thousands of cultivars, hybrids and varieties.

Thus the chrysanthemum presents an immediate contradiction in being both a shrunken genus and a rapidly expanding one, albeit expanding on the basis of an almost incestuous inclination. A recent writer on the chrysanthemum was driven to state that the number

CHRYSANTHÈMES D'AUTOMNE

1. Mr. C. ORCHARD   2. Mr. H. CANNELL

Autumnal crimson and yellow: P. de Pannemaeker, 'Chrysanthèmes d'automne', chromolithograph from Jean Linden's *L'Illustration horticole* (1886).

of cultivars 'is very unclear' and blamed multiple cultivars for a tendency to introduce a 'wild card' every so often, seized upon by breeders to try and improve hardiness or encourage a distinctive petal shape. Despite this proliferation, almost all varieties of the so-called Chinese and Japanese chrysanthemum beloved of the florist

Claude Monet, *Chrysanthemums*, 1882, oil on canvas. The vase and chrysanthemums look like pink and white clouds.

and show breeder are blended hybrids or other forms derived from *Chrysanthemum* x *morifolium* and *Chrysanthemum indicum*, both natives of eastern Asia. Although it was not until they had crossed continents with the aid of Victorian and Edwardian plant hunters that they were actually introduced to each other. Indeed in one of the first books on the chrysanthemum, the nineteenth-century breeder and nurseryman John Salter noted that

The chrysanthemum of 1865 differs so widely from the [introduced] chrysanthemum of 1764 . . . that few persons would recognise it as the same flower, for at that time all, or nearly so, of the varieties were semi-double, with quilled, or long narrow ragged florets. This will serve to give some idea of what florists had to contend with before a flower so unsightly could be moulded into the symmetrical form it now possesses . . . the wonders that man has achieved by long years of diligent and persevering effort.[1]

Sex and breeding inevitably raises its head in any discussion of fauna and flora, but the chrysanthemum also manages to introduce sexism into the mix. Chrysanthemum blooms are actually composed of many individual flowers (florets), each one capable of producing

Postcard of ox-eye daisy, once a *Chrysanthemum* but now a *Leucanthemum*.

a seed but each bearing their duties with a difference. The flower contains two types of florets, with disc florets in the centre of the bloom head and ray florets on the perimeter. In the world of botany ray florets are considered imperfect flowers, as they only possess the female productive organs and need a male to assist in reproduction, while the disc florets are considered to be 'perfect flowers', as they possess both male and female reproductive organs and can therefore have sex with themselves as well as each other. This sexual prowess may have a bearing on the unfortunate lack of smell of the chrysanthemum flower as noted by Oscar Wilde (1854–1900), who observed in his 1881 poem 'Humanitad' that 'Chrysanthemums from gilded argosy/ Unload their gaudy scentless merchandise', although that lack of scent did not prevent the novelist D. H. Lawrence (1885–1930) from writing a short story entitled 'Odour of Chrysanthemums' just thirty years later. Lawrence envisioned the chrysanthemums of the story as rather soulless and lacking in emotion, perhaps playing with the theme of absence.

The journey by which the chrysanthemum had come to the northern English coal-mining town of Lawrence's imagination had been a long one and perhaps it cannot be blamed for wilting a little on the way as it passed from the glories of Chinese dynasties, through the hands of plant hunters, to the New World and back again, before becoming the flower of choice for uninspired husbands faced with the repetitiveness of the wedding anniversary. Presumably aware of the lack of scent from the actual chrysanthemum, in 1969 the company Fabergé created a perfume named Kiku (Japanese for chrysanthemum). Marketed in bright yellow containers as a nod to the flower itself, its packaging appealed to the modern woman at a period when bright orange and yellow was widely seen in fashion and fabrics. The scent itself had nothing of the slightly bitter smell of the chrysanthemum leaf, instead being composed, in the words of its creators, of top notes of aldehydes and bergamot; middle notes of rose, lily, coconut, Tahitian gardenia, orange blossom and ylang-ylang; and base notes of sandalwood, amber, vanilla, oakmoss and

Distinctive florets on a perfect chrysanthemum head, from G. Seveyrens and P. de Longpre, *Revue horticole* (1890).

overleaf: The perfection that can be obtained by a single bloom.

musk. This mix of light floral and heavy base tones, which reads like a mad experiment in the perfume laboratory, was discontinued in 1976, but still enjoys a following on the second-hand market for both its scent and its 1970s-style packaging.

The history of the true, if scentless, chrysanthemum stretches back much further than its namesake, and takes in myths just as exotic as the perfume as it journeyed from East to West. Now one of the most important flower crops in many countries, its blooms fill florists' shops, supermarkets and less noble points of sale for seemingly 'everlasting' bouquets in the latest fashionable tones of white, yellow and lime green, the pinks and purples having fallen by the wayside in the new millennium. In the 1990s its traditional home country of Japan sold over 2 billion cut stems of chrysanthemum, with the Netherlands producing 800 million and Colombia 600 million (both of the latter largely for export). Italy, where chrysanthemums are used almost exclusively for funerals, also produces 500 million blooms – betokening either extreme generosity among mourners or a questionably high death rate, unless they too are destined for export. Despite its prime positioning as 'the flower of the Fall Season', the USA only produced 300 million cut stalks in the 1990s, although by 2009/10 the number of potted plants sold for use outdoors was 45 million, with a further 7 million destined for more cosseted indoor climes.

These figures are far in advance of what might be thought the most popular seasonal plant for America, the poinsettia, which sold only 36 million pots in the same period and is interestingly also scentless, appearance and longevity being the prime charms for the modern-day flower trade. Indeed from their arrival in Europe in the eighteenth century it has been the appearance and mutability of the chrysanthemum which has engaged florists and nurserymen in their never-ending task of turning the original Chinese flower of gold into something of more immediate monetary value. Despite the number of blooms produced, the chrysanthemum has retained its air of exoticism, lighting up a dull autumn room with startling heads of perfect symmetry and hues from perfect white to deepest purple. Placed in a Chinese vase and eschewing the practical Western names of 'Topaz', 'Pearl' or 'Orange Perfection' for the more dreamlike 'Yellow Tiger's Claw' or 'White Waves of Autumn' of its original homeland, the chrysanthemum brings together the East and the West, past and present, long life and happiness.

The beauty and simplicity of the chrysanthemum symbol, depicted on a 17th-century Edo period Japanese porcelain (Hizen ware) jar.

one

The Honourable and Imperial Flower

For his morning tea
A monk sits down in utter silence –
Confronted by chrysanthemums.
MATSUO BASHŌ (松尾 芭蕉, 1644–1694)

Asia forms the heartland of the wild chrysanthemum, with China the centre of diversity. Cultivation of the plant, with its small yellow daisy-like flowers, is recorded during the Shang Dynasty (*c.* 1600–1046 BC), and by the Tang Dynasty (AD 618–907) there were numerous varieties of chrysanthemum being grown, their differing petals and colours celebrated in Chinese literature. The later Song Dynasty (AD 960–1279) is often held to be a cultural and artistic golden age in China, and this was certainly true for chrysanthemum lovers, with doubles and multicoloured flowers appearing for the first time. By the mid-fifteenth century, when we have the first comprehensive record of Chinese chrysanthemums, there were four hundred cultivars in China in a range of colours; as many cultivars in fact as were advertised in American plant nurseries in the late nineteenth century.[1]

In addition to being prized for its beauty, the chrysanthemum was incorporated into the very heart of Chinese culture, in literature, religion and the very rhythm of the seasons, with festivals and traditions linked to their flowering. Unlike the relatively simple and largely romanticized 'language of flowers' of the West, in China the meaning of individual plants is overlaid not only with historical and cultural association and religious symbolism, but with philosophical attributes associated with flower shape, colour, flowering time and growth habit. In Chinese culture plants may also be combined to make favourable or auspicious groupings; for example the pine, bamboo and plum combine to make the 'Three Friends of Winter', or *suihan sanyou*, and represent longevity and perseverance, which in turn are virtues attached to the 'gentleman scholar'. When the chrysanthemum, bamboo, plum blossom and orchid are combined they are collectively referred to as the 'Four Gentlemen' or 'Four Noblemen'. In this guise they represent the four seasons and the unfolding nature of the year from autumn to winter through spring and summer. This in turn represents the passage through life and its cyclical return. The plum blossom is the first to bloom each year and stands for perseverance and purity, while the chrysanthemum is a symbol of autumn and preparing for dangers ahead and is thus imbued and equipped with the wisdom of age and life force of the summer now passed.

The flowering of the chrysanthemum is associated with the ninth lunar month of the year; the word *jiu* used to mean 'nine' has the same pronunciation as *jiu*, 'long-lasting', and is often used as a 'toast' at weddings to wish for a long and successful marriage. This is in turn related to the chrysanthemum through its association with the ninth month and the naming of the plant as the phonetically related *chu*. During the Han Dynasty (206 BC–AD 220), people drank chrysanthemum wine on the ninth day of the ninth lunar month in order to prolong their lives, and the drinking of chrysanthemum teas and wines became associated with health throughout the year, as well as during the annual Double Ninth Festival. In Chinese cultures 'concepts' as well as things may be allocated yin and yang (the principle of duality that all existing things have an inseparable or contrary force), six for example is a yin number, nine a yang number, and two yang numbers together are powerful and need to be balanced by other activities which contain yin. In many ways the Double Ninth Festival is therefore a double yang, both a celebration of the present and a

This modern *Chrysanthemum rubellum* commemorates its ancient past in its name, 'Emperor of China'.

cleansing to prepare for future dangers: it stands aptly at the changing of the seasons, when both physical and metaphysical hazards may occur – linked not only with the hard winter months to come but with any kind of major change. The symbolism of climbing a hill or mountain is often part of the celebrations as it evokes both climbing away from danger and making one's way through future trials. The summit of the hill and the remembrance of ancestors may be equated in the traditional poem 'Double Ninth, Remembering My Shandong Brothers' by the eighth-century Tang Dynasty poet Wang Wei (AD 699–761), who depicts the brothers wearing the red *zhuyu* (*Cornus officinalis* or Asiatic Dogwood), which is associated with the chrysanthemum on the day of the Double Ninth as they both protect against illness and hazard.

As a lonely stranger in a foreign land,
At every holiday my homesickness increases.
Far away, I know my brothers have reached the peak;
They are wearing the zhuyu, but one is not present.

Many cities and regions in China hold chrysanthemum festivals on the day of the Double Ninth, among them the Xiaolanzhen Chrysanthemum Festival in the Xiaolan area of Zhongshan, China. Legend tells that during the Song Dynasty an imperial concubine ran away from the imperial palace and travelled to the area of Xiaolan, where she found a fertile plain with a mild climate which was ideal for the growing of the court's favourite flowers. During the centuries that followed, through the Ming and the Qing dynasties, the people of the area became more adept at cultivating and training chrysanthemums and developed many colours and types. In 1736 there was the first Xiaolan 'Chrysanthemum Growing Contest' to see who could breed the best blossoms, but five years later the contest was changed to a festival so that people brought chrysanthemums to share and enjoyed writing and reading poetry about the flowers, as well as drinking chrysanthemum teas and wines. Gradually the festival developed, with more complex decorations, until in 1814 a Grand Chrysanthemum Festival was held – decorating the whole of the city and its houses. This was repeated every sixty years, in 1874, 1934 and 1994. Between those dates there were smaller festivals, often dedicated to specific themes.

In 1959 the festival for the tenth anniversary of the People's Republic of China included giant pictures created from chrysanthemums, including the Dove of Peace, 10 metres long and 7 metres high (33 × 23 ft). In 1994 almost the whole of Xiaolan was covered in chrysanthemums, with an estimated 1 million pots, as well as figurative pieces and a chrysanthemum tower. Since then the festival has included both chrysanthemum growing contests (similar to Western flower shows with individuals and societies competing to grow the best chrysanthemums) and chrysanthemum modelling exhibitions with characters, scenes, animals and buildings created from chrysanthemums. Chrysanthemum cakes, soups and drinks are also made for the occasion. A modern chrysanthemum festival is also held at Tongxiang City, in northern Zhejiang Province. The 'city' comprises nine towns and one township within three separate districts, and is

Tableaux and figures of chrysanthemums appear in both Chinese and Japanese flower festivals, such as the Ujima Jinja Chrysanthemum Festival, 2008.

what is defined as a 'county-level city'; it houses the Tongxiang World Trade Centre, which has encouraged and funded this modern festival in order to attract both trade and tourism to the area. *Hángbáijú*, a variety of chrysanthemum-flower tea, is said to originate from Tongxiang and is served at the festival.

Although the chrysanthemum itself originates in China, the concept of the chrysanthemum festival has a longer-documented history in Japan, where the plant was adopted by the eighth century, with the first imperial chrysanthemum show thought to have been held in AD 910. Flower festivals are an important part of Japanese culture as regards marking the phases of the year: starting with the Plum Blossom Festival in February and March and followed by the famous Cherry Blossom Festival (Sakura) and the Pink Moss Festivals – the last best seen at the Fuji Shibazakura Festival (near Mount Fuji) in late spring/early summer. Modern chrysanthemum festivals are spread throughout Japan, including the Shorinzan Chrysanthemum Show at the temple Daruma-ji, Takasaki City; the Bunkyo Festival at Yushima Tenjin Shrine, Tokyo; and the Okayama Castle Festival in Okayama Prefecture. In addition to the exhibitions of individual chrysanthemums in traditional tents and structures, some towns, such as Nihonmatsu, clothe their streets and buildings with chrysanthemums and build tableaux featuring figures dressed in the plants. Chrysanthemum teas and wines are drunk; small chrysanthemums are used as a garnish on foods; and chrysanthemum flowers are floated on the traditional Japanese drink sake (a rice wine), served in sake cups with chrysanthemum decoration. In Japan, the traditional timing of the festival has now been changed to occur on 9 September according to the Gregorian Calendar rather than following the traditional lunar calendar, but in China the festival date still varies each year to reflect the lunar month. In 2017 the Double Ninth Festival in China fell on the Western date of 28 October, in 2018 it was 17 October and 7 October in 2019. Celebrations for the Double Ninth now also occur in Hong Kong, Vietnam and Korea under the guise of the Chung Yeung Festival (Hong Kong) and Tết Trùng Cửu in Vietnam.

Ensuring a successful passage between past and future has marked out the celebration of the Double Ninth as also being an auspicious date for tidying and decorating the graves of ancestors. Flowers and traditional foods are left for the ancestors, or dedicated to them and then eaten by the living. Recently the celebration has also been designated 'Senior Citizens Day' in Taiwan, making official the tradition of bringing gifts to the elderly and celebrating age and longevity, symbols also incorporated in the chrysanthemum with its long-lived flowers. Less promising for a long life is the traditional Japanese story of the two brothers who promised to meet each other on the day of the chrysanthemum festival. One was thrown into prison, but so determined was he to keep his promise that he took his own life in order that his spirit might be free to return. So it happened that, as his brother waited by a vase of chrysanthemums, the freed spirit came to him on the evening breeze to keep its mortal promise.[2]

Immortality is also said to await those who drink from the crystal-clear river that flows beside a river in Kai, Japan. On the hill above grow chrysanthemums whose petals fall into the clear waters below and endow the waters and all who drink there with everlasting life.[3]

Despite originating in China, the chrysanthemum has become embedded in Western images of Japan, as this 1910 image by Elizabeth Gordon attests.

FLOWER CHILDREN

CHRYSANTHEMUM is Japanese,
She 's a fine lady, if you please;
She comes to see us once a year,
About the time Thanksgiving 's here.

There is a legend that the original 'golden daisies of the Orient' first arrived in Japan from China in a boat washed ashore on an island in the Japanese archipelago. Within the boat were twelve maidens and twelve boys, carrying a precious cargo of chrysanthemums which they were to trade for the Japanese herb of youth in order to save the life of their revered Chinese emperor. Finding the island uninhabited, the travellers settled down to build an empire and plant the chrysanthemums. As legends often do, this one contains both elements of truth and unanswered mysteries. The story correctly puts the birthplace of chrysanthemums in China and also rather neatly explains the tradition that the flowers were for centuries the exclusive possession of the Japanese emperor. What it does not clarify is what exactly the herb of youth was and why they were expecting to trade it for the flower of longevity. And indeed what happened to the anxious

Chrysanthemum tea is part of the Japanese chrysanthemum festival tradition,
as well as being generally imbibed for good health.

Chinese emperor waiting back at home once the travellers abandoned
their quest?

However, once in Japan, by whatever means, the chrysanthemum
was embedded in the heart of the cultural and political system. In
the twelfth century the Japanese emperor Go-Toba (1180–1239) took
the flower as his personal imperial symbol, and by the late thirteenth
century it had become the official flower and symbol of the royal family, who from then onwards were said to inhabit the Chrysanthemum
Throne. In the castle of Osaka in Kyoto, constructed by the Japanese
leader Toyotomi Hideyoshi (1536/7–1598), is an apartment known
as the Chrysanthemum Room or the *Kiku-no-ma*, which was used as
a waiting room for guests. It is decorated with yellow and white chrysanthemums and autumn grasses on a gold background, all painted
by Kaiho Yusetsu (1598–1677). Yusetsu also decorated the veranda
and ceiling with fans, while the doors of the room depict a cat asleep
under peonies on one side and a willow tree and herons on the other
side are by the artist Kano Ryotaku. Soon everything associated with
the rule of the country, from money to warships, had the chrysanthemum symbol embossed or printed upon it. A simplified eight- or

Torii Kiyonaga, *A Young Woman with a Dog*, Edo period, c. 1790–91, polychrome woodblock print; ink and colour on paper.

sixteen-petalled flower emblem was also used to decorate ceramics and textiles, while paintings of the real chrysanthemum were central to both Chinese and Japanese art.

Holding a special place in Chinese art painting and poetry was the scholar-poet Du Jin (*c.* 1465–1509). Du Jin was the son of an official and expected to follow his father dutifully into a career dedicated to governance, but a disappointing performance in the metropolitan (*jinshi*) examination led him to another career instead – as a painter and poet. Adept at portraying both landscapes and figures, Du Jin worked in an academic style and, like so many contemporaries, hovered between scholar and artist – an ideal position for the painter of a flower as symbolic as the chrysanthemum. Du Jin's painting *Tao Yuanming Enjoying Chrysanthemums* portrays the poet Tao Qian (365–427) admiring autumn flowers and yellow chrysanthemums while on a mountain walk (his servant is shown holding some flowers). An accompanying verse includes these lines: 'Along three paths he returned, at leisure with his bramble staff,/ The sun moved west over the yellow flowers and wattle fence.'

The sombre tone of the painting of Tao Qian contrasts with the bright red chrysanthemum-covered silks of the women of the artist

Postcards such as this were designed to lure visitors to Japan in the early 20th century.

Torii Kiyonaga (1752–1815). Also renowned for his portraits of actors, Torii Kiyonaga wrapped one beautiful woman in bright silk robes. Her red outer robe is decorated with chrysanthemum roundels in delicate colours, her *furisode* (a kimono with long, swinging sleeves) of peach silk has orchid designs, and the cream under-robe and red undergarment add to the contrast with her black *obi* or sash. Tall, stately and slightly remote, the subject can be identified as a woman of high standing. The classical twofold screen behind her, decorated with a closed blind, further removes her from everyday life. Anchoring her spreading robes to the floor is a Japanese spaniel, a creature that, like its mistress, was prized for elegance. The eighteenth-century Japanese artist Utagawa Kuniyoshi (1798–1861) also depicted the association between beautiful Japanese women and the chrysanthemum, creating a series of at least seventeen images inscribed with women's actions or thoughts, and the chrysanthemum variety that might be associated with that. Called the 'Imayô kiku-zoroi', or 'An Assortment of Chrysanthemums in the Modern Style', the prints were produced by several different publishers around 1845. Collected by museums worldwide, including the V&A Museum in London, they formed part of a publication by that museum in 1961,[4] and are now also part of an online study of over 5,000 images of Kuniyoshi's work. Their bringing together of women and chrysanthemums is a theme that runs through Japanese art and culture and can be seen for example in the postcards that promoted tourism to Japan in the early twentieth century. Kuniyoshi also created the stunning image *Chrysanthemums of One Hundred Varieties Grafted Together*, shown overleaf.

It was during the Edo period in Japan (1603–1868) that the chrysanthemum became the subject of one of the most important Japanese artists of all time, Katsushika Hokusai. Born in Edo (now Tokyo), Hokusai (1760–1849) is best known both in Japan and in the West for his woodblock print series 'Thirty-six Views of Mount Fuji', which includes the iconic print *The Great Wave off Kanagawa*. The 'Thirty-six Views of Mount Fuji' were part of Hokusai's personal obsession with Mount Fuji, and the 'Great Wave' became a statement

Utagawa Kuniyoshi, *Chrysanthemums of One Hundred Varieties Grafted Together* (*Hyakushu tsugiwake-giku*), 1843–7, woodblock print; ink and colour on paper.

of art and philosophy combined that travelled the world. Apprenticed to a wood-carver until the age of eighteen, Hokusai worked under various names as his art transitioned from traditional depictions of courtesans and Kabuki actors towards plants and landscapes. His detailed individual images of flowers and birds are often created with a movement and perspective which marry Western and Eastern art and the images were influential for the European Impressionist movement, as well as transforming art in the later Edo period.

Chrysanthemums formed just one small part of Hokusai's artistic output but his depictions are some of the most exquisite and detailed images of this flower known in Japan. The woodcut *Chrysanthemums and Horsefly* (from the series 'Large Flowers'), dated to around 1830, depicts in detail both incurved and fine-petalled flowers in subtle arrays of pinks, oranges and yellows, while *Iris, Hydrangea, Pinks and Chrysanthemums* of 25 years earlier depicts the small yellow/brown Chusan daisy-style chrysanthemum among the other more flamboyant flowers. *People Viewing Chrysanthemum Exhibit* (1799) draws back from the detail of the flowers to give us an image of old Japan with elaborately coiffured geishas and a man flicking insects (or heat?) away from the flowers in a show marking the ninth-month festival of chrysanthemums. The symbol of the chrysanthemum as marking longevity of body and mind is a perfect symbol for Katsushika Hokusai's own statement on art and life:

> From the age of six, I had a passion for copying the form of things and since the age of fifty I have published many drawings, yet of all I drew by my seventieth year there is nothing worth taking into account. At seventy-three years I partly understood the structure of animals, birds, insects and fishes, and the life of grasses and plants. And so, at eighty-six I shall progress further; at ninety I shall even further penetrate their secret meaning, and by one hundred I shall perhaps truly have reached the level of the marvellous and divine. When I am one hundred and ten, each dot, each line will possess a life of its own.[5]

Katsushika Hokusai, *Sparrows and Chrysanthemums*, c. 1825, polychrome woodblock print; ink and colour on paper.

Born slightly later than Hokusai, and considered by many as the last great master of *ukiyo-e* art is Utagawa Hiroshige (1797–1858). Hiroshige combined duties as a fire-warden for the Yayosu Quay area (a duty handed down from his father) with work as an artist and was extremely prolific, producing thousands of pieces, although he never achieved financial success. Concentrating on depictions of flowers and birds, Hiroshige is thought to have been influenced by Hokusai's 'Thirty-six Views of Mount Fuji', producing his own series 'The Fifty-three Stations of the Tōkaidō' and 'The Sixty-nine Stations of the Kiso Kaidō'. His works included many depicting the chrysanthemum, plum blossom and iris, as well as landscapes and the seasons. In 1856 Hiroshige became a Buddhist monk and retired from the world, dying aged 62 during the great Edo cholera epidemic of 1858 (although his actual cause of death is unknown). He was buried in a Zen Buddhist temple in Asakusa, concluding his life with the poem:

Utagawa Hiroshige, *Chrysanthemums in Fan-shaped Design*, 1840s, polychrome woodblock print; ink and colour on paper.

I leave my brush in the East
And set forth on my journey.
I shall see the famous places in the Western Land.

For an empire that fell in love with the chrysanthemum at first sight it seems ironic that the Japanese were also responsible for altering both its form and its shape to such an extent that it became almost unrecognizable from that early flower that made the journey across the seas from China. Pioneering different forms of cultivation and selection, including removal of side shoots, Japanese florists were able to greatly increase the size of the flower-head as well as the forms of the petals. The first Japanese text on chrysanthemum cultivation and types appeared in 1717, around three hundred years after the first Chinese text on the flower, but with a vastly increased number of flower shapes and types.

One late nineteenth-century American article (translated from original French) records these Japanese cultivars as achieving up to 20 centimetres (8 in.) in diameter, with bamboo tubes needed to hold up the heavy single blooms for exhibition, although the writer concludes that such novelties might as well be made from paper as they appeared to him to bear little relation to real flowers.[6] Types included 'Saga', with narrow petals and a delicate loose head; 'Edo' (named after the city), with medium-sized flowers but petals which kinked back over the centre of the flower itself, memorably described by the writer Noel Kingsbury as 'like a punk version of a comb-over'; 'The Sacred Ise', with narrow hanging petals, often with split ends, best appreciated by looking up at them from below; 'Osyu', or the 'great fist', with heavy twisted outer petals which need support and closely curled inner ones; and 'Higo' themselves – the simplest of the flowers, with narrow petals but an accompanying complexity of rules regarding their growing and showing.[7]

In 1880 the diplomat Ernest Mason Satow (1843–1929) recorded in his diary for 18 November:

Mikado's chrysanthemum garden party. The weather was magnificent and the flowers beautiful. Particularly worthy of remark were six bushes, at least five feet in diameter, on a single stalk and completely covered in flowers.[8]

Satow obviously had an eye for flowers. Years earlier he had noted on one of his first diplomatic calls: 'Went to see Ohara Shuntaro's chrysanthemums in the afternoon. They were very beautiful, especially one yellow species with delicate golden florets, like a star with a myriad rays.'[9] In 1871, while visiting flower nurseries in Sugamo, Tokyo, he admired the chrysanthemum shows there, recording:

> In one was an enormous *gaku* [scene or tableaux] twelve feet long by six high entirely composed of chrysanthemums, with the character *kotobuki* [good luck] written or embroidered on it in pink blossoms. The roots were entirely concealed, and this sort of frame appeared to be suspended in the air. There was a group of two ladies and a boy, whose dresses were entirely formed of maroon blossoms with an edging of yellow marks and hands of painted wood apparently.[10]

As a diplomat serving in Japan, Satow was never able to marry his Japanese common-law wife, Takeda Kane (1853–1932), but their relationship was nevertheless recognized and their second son, Takeda Hisayoshi, became a noted botanist, studying at Kew in the early part of his career.

As well as expanding the size and type of blooms, the overall shape of the Japanese chrysanthemum was altered by constant training to produce, among other types, the popular Japanese 'waterfall' or 'bridge' styles – where a miniaturized plant is trained over a bamboo framework to produce a cascade of flowers, or a single plant is made to produce a thousand blooms, or combine several varieties.

Such methods of extreme cultivation were also used in China and Hong Kong, as reported in detail in the British periodical *My Garden* in 1934. A Chinese gardener hired by one Mr Bagram produced magnificent 'trees' of over 250 chrysanthemum blooms by pegging down individual side shoots and encouraging the growth of laterals, which were then fed and disbudded to leave one perfect bloom. This pampered but solitary flower was then tied to a bamboo stake and placed in faultless symmetry with the other 249 blooms to produce a perfect pyramid. Although the writer in *My Garden* could not help but admire the cascade chrysanthemums with their 'tiny stars in a floral torrent from ceiling to floor of the greenhouse' she was much less impressed by the effigies and figures produced for the annual chrysanthemum spectacles, which 'have little to appeal to British taste', cloying the senses 'even as it fascinates'. That Eastern growers were said to be able to produce up to a thousand flowers on each plant was, the writer grudgingly admitted, 'a magnificent sight', but what mattered more to the British gardener was 'the quality of individual sprays and flowers' rather than the size or form of a plant.

Quality over quantity was the English way and although amateur growers were told to follow the Eastern practice of frequent feeding,

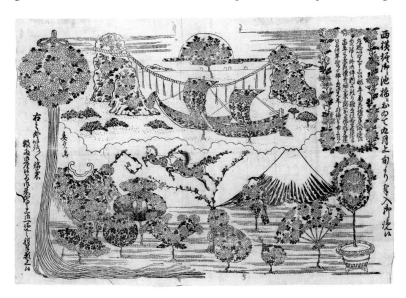

Yasukawa Harusada I, *Chrysanthemum Topiaries*, 1844, woodblock print; ink on paper.

it was made clear that it was carried out for very different aims. When it came to the appearance of the individual chrysanthemum flowers, however, there was no doubt that the various Japanese types, bizarre though they were to Western eyes, had a mystique all of their own. The tasselled, fringed, curled or crumpled petals, the ragged ribbons and fluffy spheres, struck a dual chord with the chrysanthemum admirer – all being composed of the two types of floret on the head of every chrysanthemum: the ray floret and the tubular floret. Even more poetic were the Japanese names for the cultivars: 'Dye of the Dew', 'Waves in the Morning Sun', 'Moon's Halo' and 'Shadows of the Evening Sun' were all admired in *My Garden*, putting the rather more mundane Western cultivars 'Ethel', 'White Midget', 'Henry E. Truemann' (also white) and even the crimson 'Mrs A. Holden' in the shade. The anemone-flowered 'Thora', a popular inter-war chrysanthemum, had a 'lovely circle of rosy rays enclosing a prominent cream

The modern chrysanthemum display has changed little from the images and postcards of the early 19th century.

centre' but somehow even that faded against the prospect of a chrysanthemum named after 'waves in the morning sun'.[11] Although these elaborate flowers were favoured for Japanese shows, it was the simple, small-flowered chrysanthemum that was still used for decoration in traditional tea ceremonies, such that early photographs of Western tourists in Japan often depict these simpler flowers as though centuries of Japanese chrysanthemum breeding had never taken place.

By the late nineteenth century so varied were the shapes and colours of the Japanese chrysanthemum that the Edwardian chrysanthemum specialist Arthur Herrington recorded: 'Although a blue rose may be an impossibility . . . we are told that a variety of the chrysanthemum exists in Japan with blue flowers.'[12] Herrington may have been rather gullible, as he based his information largely on the presence of blue chrysanthemums on Kyō Satsuma porcelain. Traditionally produced in the Kyoto area and known for its gorgeous colours, meticulous technique and ornately detailed painting, Kyō Satsuma wares were first developed just before and during the early Meiji period (1868–1912). They astounded Westerners at the Paris International Exhibition of 1867 and the Vienna International Exhibition of 1873, where vases, incense burners, bowls and dishes included gold, red and blue chrysanthemums. They quickly found their way into collections, including those of some of the foremost museums and galleries of Europe and America, such as the V&A (London), the Guimet Museum of Asian Art in France and the Philadelphia Museum of Art.

However, in addition to these 'mythical' chrysanthemum images there is a written reference to a blue chrysanthemum in the *History of [the Reign of] Nin-toku-ten-wau.* This states that

> In 386, in the seventy-third year of his reign, seeds of the chrysanthemum were introduced into Japan from a foreign country [the kingdom of Paiktse, a state of Korea], both blue, yellow, red, white and violet.[13]

The bluey mauve chrysanthemum on this early 20th-century postcard owes something to the imagination.

This colourful image contradicts both the accepted date for the first introduction of the chrysanthemum into Japan (in the eighth century) and the accepted colour range of the chrysanthemum at that date, but is a delightful if mythical floral addition to the story of an emperor who is otherwise now mainly remembered for his extraordinarily large mausoleum in the city of Sakai. The tomb covers about 120,775 square metres (1.3 million sq. ft) and is said to have taken 800,000 labourers twenty years to build. Creating a blue chrysanthemum might have been seen as a simple task in comparison.

It may have been dishes such as these with their glittering glazes and chrysanthemum decoration that were referred to in the legend of the maiden O-Kiku (Chrysanthemum). O-Kiku was working as a dishwashing maid in the town of Go-Ken-Yashiki and was put in charge of ten dishes made of gold. One day a dish was missing and O-Kiku, fearful of suspicion, threw herself into a well. Ever since, the 'ghost' of little O-Kiku counts the golden dishes from one to nine – 'Ichi-mai, Ni-mai, San-mai, Yo-mai, Go-mai, Roku-mai, Shichi-mai, Hachi-mi, Ku-mai' – and then weeps wretchedly over the missing tenth dish before beginning the count again. That is why, it is said,

The Japanese
Order of the
Chrysanthemum,
established
in 1876, reflects
the deep hold that
this flower has on
Japanese culture.

it is thought unlucky to cultivate chrysanthemums in Go-Ken-Yashiki, which must be a blow to its flower-loving inhabitants anxious to follow in Japanese tradition.[14]

In 1876, in order to honour both the chrysanthemum and members of the imperial court, Emperor Meiji, the 122nd emperor of Japan, created the Supreme Order of the Chrysanthemum or the Dai-kun'i kikka-shō (loosely, the Grand Order of the Chrysanthemum, but more literally the Grand Order of the Capitulum of the Chrysanthemums). This 'order' is signified by the wearing of a chrysanthemum medal, although a further embellishment of the order made several years later permitted the wearer to add either a chain (with collar) or wear the medal 'with grand cordon', which is a form of sash, while a further complication was added later where the single petals on the medal might be shown as double. The award was more or less exclusive to members of the imperial family, and in the 150 years since its creation only seven Japanese citizens have been given the chrysanthemum order, although it is now a favourite honour awarded to foreign heads of state during a visit to Japan.

So indivisible from the culture of Japan is the chrysanthemum that when the anthropologist Ruth Benedict (1887–1948) wrote her seminal work on modern Japanese culture, she entitled it *The Chrysanthemum and the Sword: Patterns of Japanese Culture* to reflect the duality of Japan and the ties to tradition that pervaded all social actions and relationships, both military and cultural. Benedict was made president of the American Anthropological Association for her work in anthropology and folklore and was the first woman to be recognized as a prominent leader of that profession. Her work in general explored the connection between culture and the individual and emphasized that understanding traditional cultures could help us understand modern man; this approach became an influential motif for anthropology in the 1930s and 1950s. As well as studying Japanese culture, Benedict undertook studies of peoples in the American Southwest and worked alongside Margaret Mead (1901–1978), famous for her study and publication of *Coming of Age in Samoa* (1928),

Yoshu (Hashimoto) Chikanobu, *Emperor Meiji, His Wife, and Prince Haru*, 1887, triptych of polychrome woodblock prints; ink and colour on paper. The emperor wears the Order of the Chrysanthemum.

Ruth Benedict, author of *The Chrysanthemum and the Sword* (1946), wearing coincidentally what appears to be a loose imitation of a silk chrysanthemum.

as well as the German-American Franz Boas (1858–1942), who founded the school of anthropological historicism to which Benedict's study belonged.

Seemingly a piece of pure research, *The Chrysanthemum and the Sword* was in fact written at the invitation of the U.S. Office of War Information in order to understand and predict the behaviour of the Japanese in the Second World War by reference to the seeming contradictions in their traditional culture. The Japanese, Benedict wrote, are

> both aggressive and unaggressive, both militaristic and aesthetic, both insolent and polite, rigid and adaptable, submissive and resentful of being pushed around, loyal and treacherous, brave and timid, conservative and hospitable to new ways.[15]

517—A Chrysanthemum Secret, Japan.
Copyright 1906, by W. S. Smith.

Traditionally dressed, these women wear the same flowers that surround them, 1905, photographic print on stereo card.

Her book was influential in shaping American ideas about the Japanese way of life for many decades, and despite modern caveats regarding her approach and findings, the phrase 'chrysanthemum and sword' has remained a form of shorthand to refer to the history of Japanese politics and culture. The book itself was translated into Japanese in 1948, becoming in turn an influence on the way the Japanese saw themselves in relation to Western culture; it also became a bestseller in the People's Republic of China when relations with Japan soured in 2005. As a political force the chrysanthemum and the sword have a longer history as well as a continued presence. For example, in 1906 it was the chrysanthemum that was chosen to be depicted on a stone marking the boundary between Japan and Russia in the disputed territories of Sakhalin; on his father's death in January 1989, the 125th emperor, Emperor Akihito, acceded – as his forefathers had done before him – to the Chrysanthemum Throne; and the Japanese passport still retains a chrysanthemum symbol as a constant reminder of personal adherence to the tradition of all that the flower represents.

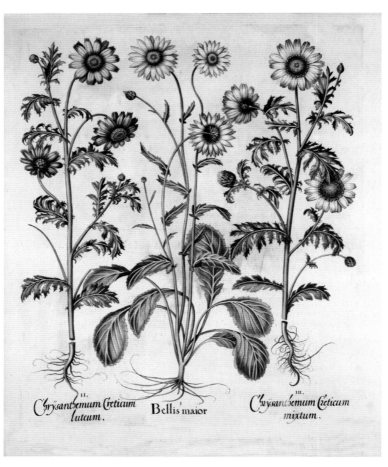

Chrysanthemum creticum luteum and *Chrysanthemum creticum mixtum* depicted in Basilius
Besler's *Hortus Eystettensis* (1613).

two

Smuggling Tea and Chrysanthemums

𝕏

In 1796 William Curtis (1746–1799), botanical writer and editor of the *Botanical Magazine*, widely known as *Curtis's Botanical Magazine*, announced in that publication the arrival in England of the ornamental and highly valuable acquisition for all flower fanciers, the 'Indian' chrysanthemum or (in the classical language of botanists) the *Chrysanthemum indicum*. Setting aside the casual manner in which plants from 'the East' were regularly assigned to some mythical all-encompassing 'India', it seems almost incredible that the flower so beloved of the East had not made its way to England prior to the late eighteenth century. However, that is exactly what Curtis went on to suggest and although there has subsequently been some confusion over 'when is a chrysanthemum not a chrysanthemum', Curtis's claim to have been the herald of the first true florists' chrysanthemum on English soil remains largely unchallenged and oft repeated. In fact flowers named 'chrysanthemum' had been described in the numerous 'herbals' and 'plant histories' well before the eighteenth century, as might be expected given that the term literally meant 'gold flower'. Basilius Besler, in his *Hortus Eystettensis* of 1613, also laid claim to chrysanthemums growing in the garden of the Bishop of Eichstätt in Bavaria. However, the chrysanthemums recorded by Besler (1561–1629) are those which were native to Europe, such as the *Chrysanthemum creticum luteum* and the rather confused *Chrysanthemum creticum mixtum*, which are not the true florists' chrysanthemum of Asia but are instead related to the corn marigold (now classified as

Glebionis segetum but once *Chrysanthemum segetum*). The great herbals or plant histories of John Gerard and John Parkinson also referred to the 'Peruvian Chrysanthemum', which was, as both the description and illustration clearly show, nothing more or less than the statuesque South American sunflower.

In 1688 the scientist and naturalist Jacob Breyne or Bryen (sometimes Latinized to Breynius or Breynii) (1637–1697) carefully recorded in his catalogue of rare plants observed in the gardens of Holland chrysanthemums in colours of Rosige, Weiße, Purpurne, Gelbe, Fleischfarbige und Kupfrige (rose, white, purple, yellow, flesh-coloured and copper-coloured).[1] Given that the Netherlands had been trading with Japan since 1609, and that Breyne was well connected with travellers and merchants, the claim seemed to many early historians to be eminently reasonable and was often repeated in nineteenth-century journals such as the delightfully named *The Wanderer* (December 1894 edition).

Henry Phillips's *Flora Historica* (1824) records that the chrysanthemum was first introduced into England in 1754 (more than forty years before its announcement in *Curtis's Botanical Magazine*). Noting that it arrived not via the Dutch but direct from the 'Celestial Empire', Phillips claims that it was first cultivated in England by the chief gardener of the Chelsea Physic Garden, Philip Miller (1691–1771). Nonetheless, an alternative version of the chrysanthemum story contends that Miller received the *Chrysanthemum indicum* from Peter Osbeck, a student of Carl Linnaeus, who had found it near Macao in southern China and sent it back to Europe.[2] Arthur Herrington (1866–1950), writer and historian of both the chrysanthemum and the lily, dismissed the claim of either the Netherlands or Bavaria to be the first chrysanthemum country in Europe, stating that if it were so then 'certainly by 1821 no gardener in Holland knew anything of them.'[3]

Miller was said to have 'raised the reputation of the Chelsea Garden so much that it excels all the gardens of Europe for its amazing variety of plants of all orders and classes and from all climates', and by corresponding with botanists, nurseries and plant hunters across the globe, he obtained a collection of 'exotics' far in advance of anything seen before, including gaining the chrysanthemum from Nimpu on the Chinese/Bhutan border.[4] Miller was the foremost botanist and botanical writer of his day. His *Gardeners Dictionary: Containing the Best and Newest Methods of Cultivating and Improving the Kitchen, Fruit, Flower Garden, and Nursery*, first published in 1731 (and therefore sadly lacking the chrysanthemum), was to run to eight expanded editions and be translated into Dutch and French for the benefit of those plant-loving nations. Praised for his diligence, his superb plantsmanship and his ability to acquire new plants and maintain them, the only thing one can say against Philip Miller is that he appears to have 'lost' the chrysanthemum as quickly as he gained it. How this happened is not known and is described in most books that refer to the 'Miller version' of the chrysanthemum story as having been 'by some unfortunate accident'. This conjures up visions of a heavy weight falling on the plant, or neglected watering and a slow decline, but probably just means no one knows what happened. The suffering chrysanthemum may, however, have been content to know that Miller himself had the indignity of having a portrait of an entirely different 'Miller' being placed in the frontispiece of a 1787 edition of his most famous work, *The Gardeners Dictionary*, perhaps also by 'unfortunate accident'.[5]

And so we edge ever closer to that mythical date of 1796. A further delay while the chrysanthemum makes 'footfall' and then dallies for a short while in Paris, courtesy of one Pierre-Louis Blanchard. According to the original historian of the chrysanthemum, Professor Frederick William Burbidge of Dublin (and the more recent histories recorded by Judith Taylor in her book *An Abundance of Flowers: More Great Flower Breeders of the Past*), Blanchard, or possibly Blancard, was not a botanist but a sea captain of Marseille, or perhaps a merchant sailor. Merchants and sailors of the period, whether flower fanciers or not, had their eyes on likely plants that might attract a good price. Blanchard brought specimens of the chrysanthemum direct from China, and although only a few survived he is said to have distributed them to likely plant fanciers, including one Abbé de Ramatuelle, who in turn sent some to the Jardin du Roi in Paris in 1790. They also appeared around that date at the nurseries of a Monsieur Cels in Paris – some say via Blanchard's original specimens; some say from an alternative source – before making their final Channel crossing to reach the London nurseries and the attention of William Curtis in 1795 and thence to be brought at last to the wider public the following February. However, even then there is a mystery. The 'newly arrived' plant celebrated in Curtis's *Botanical Magazine* of 1796 was labelled as *Chrysanthemum indicum* (later renamed *Chrysanthemum sinensis*).[6] *C. indicum* has a single yellow flower, whereas the one illustrated by Curtis is plainly the deep purple *Chrysanthemum morifolium* (as also noted by Margaret Willes in her book on *Gardens of the British Working Class*).[7] However, given the revolution and wars raging at the time of Blanchard's discoveries it is a miracle that any plant survived at all, let alone was correctly identified when it finally reached its destination.

And so, finally, we return to the first-ever description of the chrysanthemum in England, by that worthy botanist and recorder of all things new and exotic, William Curtis. The purpose of the *Botanical Magazine* which Curtis had set up was to bring to the attention of its subscribers 'The most ornamental foreign plants, cultivated in the open ground, green-house, and the stove . . . actually represented in their true colours' and the magazine was, and indeed still is, essential reading for all flower fanciers and botanists. In his three-page description of the chrysanthemum William Curtis covered, as much as he could given its (probable) recent finding of the origin, the history and development of the chrysanthemum. He also described its cultivation and where it could be obtained by any gardeners who were eager to share in its delights. In his anxiety to trace its possible origins, Curtis attempted to match the plant to descriptions of other chrysanthemum-like plants in previous classical and historic botanical works, a standard exercise which was fraught with difficulties of both translation and the interpretation of often poor-quality drawings in

Pub by W. Curtis S.ᵗ Geo: Crescent Feb.1.1796

The first image of a florists' chrysanthemum in England, from *Curtis's Botanical Magazine*
(1795–6).

[327]

CHRYSANTHEMUM INDICUM. INDIAN
CHRYSANTHEMUM.

❋❋❋❋❋❋❋❋❋❋❋❋❋❋❋❋❋❋❋❋

Clafs and Order.

SYNGENESIA POLYGAMIA SUPERFLUA.

Generic Character.

Recept. nudum. *Pappus* marginatus. *Cal.* hemifphæricus,
imbricatus : fquamis marginalibus membranaceis.

Specific Character and Synonyms.

CHRYSANTHEMUM *indicum* foliis fimplicibus ovatis fi-
nuatis angulatis ferratis acutis. *Linn.*
Syft. Vegetab. ed. 14. *Murr. p.* 773.
Spec. Pl. 1253. *Thunb. Jap. p.* 320.
TSJETTI-PU. *Rheed. Mal. t.* 44.
MATRICARIA finenfis. *Rumph. Amb. p.* 259. *t.* 91.
MATRICARIA japonica maxima flore rofco five fuave
rubente pleno elegantiffimo. *Breyn.*
Prod. p. 66 ?
KIK, KIKF, vel KIKKU. *Kæmpf. Amæn. Ex. p.* 875.

We rejoice in the opportunity afforded us, of prefenting our
readers with the coloured engraving of a plant recently introduced to this country, which, as an ornamental one, promifes
to become an acquifition highly valuable.
This magnificent fpecies of Chryfanthemum, which we have
hitherto feen only in the collection of Mr. COLVILL, Nurfery-
man, King's-Road, Chelfea, began to flower with him early
in November laft, 1795 ; and as there were many buds on the
plant, at that time, yet unopened, it appeared as if it would
continue to flower during the early part of the winter at leaft.
It is a plant of ftrong growth ; the ftem rifing to the height
of two or three feet, fomewhat woody, much branched, befet
with numerous leaves, having fome refemblance to thofe of
Mugwort, of a greyifh hue ; the flowers, on being fmelt to,
difcover an agreeable fragrance, they are produced on the
fummits of the branches in a loofe fort of clufter (thofe which
terminate the main ftem, grow to the fize of a large carnation)
of a dark purple colour ; they are, it is to be obferved, double,
or

William Curtis's
description of the
Chrysanthemum indicum
from *Curtis's Botanical
Magazine* (1795–6).

early herbals. Citing such luminaries of the botanical world as Carl
Linnaeus and Georg Eberhard Rumphius (a seventeenth-century
botanist with the Dutch East India Company who battled through
earthquake, flood, fire, shipwreck and blindness to finish his *Herbarium
amboinense*, posthumously published in 1741), Curtis dedicated half
of the first page of description to every name under which the chrysanthemum might have been known in the past, from his own use of
Chrysanthemum indicum to a possible earlier equivalent, *Matricaria sinensis*,
and the 'native' Japanese *Kik*, *Kiku* or *Kikku* or the *Tsjetti-pu* in Malabar.
It was here that Curtis also inadvertently introduced several of the
possible 'red herrings' which have been detailed above, including

equating his chrysanthemum with the *Matricaria japonica maxima flore roseo sive suave rubento pleno elegantissimo* of Jacob Breyne or Breynius (the man himself ironically abbreviated as Breyn. Prod.).

Perhaps wisely, Curtis moved swiftly on from this confusion of nomenclature and histories to confidently introduce the plant 'recently introduced into this country' and declare it as an ornamental flower promising to become a highly valuable acquisition. Only available at the nurseries of Mr Colville in London, on Chelsea's Kings Road, it had flowered there for the first time in November 1795, marking it out as one of the very late hardy chrysanthemums. Indeed Curtis went on to say that even in the November there had been many unopened buds awaiting their turn which would flower into the winter. Multi-branched off a single stem and with leaves 'having some resemblance to those of Mugwort', the flowers were a dark purple colour and their exact petal arrangement led Curtis to suggest that the plant might merit a change of classification almost immediately from *Chrysanthemum* to *Anthemis* (a genus within the daisy family which is similar to chamomile or mayweed). Curtis identified the origin of the new flowering plant as China, where, he recorded rather vaguely, it had been cultivated 'for ages'. The Chinese, he said, had been noted by Western travellers to hold the chrysanthemum in 'high estimation', paying great attention to its culture. Grown in pots and jars, it was used to decorate the windows of their houses and apartments and brought onto dining tables when guests were entertained. This he contrasted with the rather lackadaisical approach of both the 'natives' and the Dutch in the 'East Indees', as they were known. Here he said the plants were set in sandy soil and did not set flower or seed well, in part due to the fact that their flowering coincided with the rainy season. Perhaps due to this approach, only two colours were common in the Indees, with the third (the deep-red or purple chrysanthemum that had now also made its way to England) being rare.

In China, however, a fourth variety was known (according to Curtis), with greenish-coloured flowers; although in a moment of self-doubt he queries this in his *Botanical Magazine* entry with a sort

菊の泉温スルカ島中崎長
Chrysanthemum of Nakashima, Hot Spring, Nagasaki.

Chrysanthemum show in an area of Nagasaki, once famous for its chrysanthemum nurseries.

of 'note to self' wondering whether this was not one of the varieties illustrated in the *Hortus Malabaricus* by Hendrik van Rheede (published in parts between 1678 and 1693). Taking his information from Rumphius, Curtis details the ideal form of this chrysanthemum in China as being kept dwarfish by cutting, with large blooms thinned out while in bud so that 'by this and other management they cause the flowers to grow to the breadth of one's hand.' A fifth sort of chrysanthemum, with white-blushed flowers that hung downwards in the morning and evening, was said to be extremely rare, even within China, and was not exported to other countries. Curtis seems to even doubt its existence, although he recorded its apposite name of *Tchuy say si*, or 'the drunken woman'.

Moving on to Japan, still a little-known country when Curtis was writing, he calls on the *Flora Japonica* of Carl Peter Thunberg (1784) to remark on the beauty of the chrysanthemum types in that empire, with extreme variation in colour, size and plenitude. Curtis's note that chrysanthemum-growing is especially famed in the area of Papenberg, near Nagasaki, immediately strikes twenty-first-century readers with the contrast between the beauty of the chrysanthemum and the devastation later wrought on that city.[8]

Changeable Pale Buff Chrysanthemum

In 1826 the *Transactions of the Horticultural Society of London* included the 'Changeable Pale Buff Chrysanthemum', which may be related to the 'Buff Flowered' listed by John Claudius Loudon in 1822.

Having cautiously welcomed the plant into the country, Curtis finishes by tentatively suggesting that although it is currently being grown in the hardy greenhouses of Colville's nursery, he has every hope that it will prove hardy to the mild winters that England was then experiencing and would be able to be planted out to enliven the autumn and early winter flowerbed. However, with such tardy flowering, seeds were not to be expected and so propagation must be done by cutting and 'parting of the roots'. Perhaps here lies the cause of Philip Miller's unfortunate accidental loss of the first English chrysanthemums. Before moving on from William Curtis it should be noted that, in 1821, the geographically incorrect naming of C. *indicum* was ousted from that nomenclature to become C. *sinensis*, following a somewhat heated debate in the pages of the *Transactions of the Linnean Society* in 1821.[9] This naming was used throughout the nineteenth and early twentieth century, but it was to be the first of many name changes.

As with all rarities, the chrysanthemum was at first only available to the wealthy, as prices reflected the difficulties of obtaining the plant, especially as it was not possible to create seed. But as prices dropped it became a focus for the ever-diligent 'florists' or plant fanciers, who began to experiment with obtaining different varieties and colours. Increasing from a mere nine or ten varieties in England in 1806, in 1822 John Claudius Loudon recorded that Joseph Sabine of the Horticultural Society of London knew of fourteen varieties. These rather uninspiringly named plants included 'Buff-flowered', 'Golden-flowered', 'Pink-flowered', 'Quilled Flamed Yellow', 'Quilled White', 'Sulphur Yellow', 'Tasselled White', 'Changeable White', 'Large Lilac', 'Quilled Pink', 'Quilled Yellow', 'Spanish Brown', 'Superb White' and 'The Purple'.[10] By 1825 this had increased to 48 varieties thanks to collections made in China by a Mr Parks of the Horticultural Society. The Horticultural Society (not yet Royal) kept its own collection at the Society's gardens, then in Chiswick, where it was claimed that more than seven hundred chrysanthemum plants were displayed in pots.[11]

In 1824 Henry Phillips listed the chrysanthemum as one of the plants ideal for the autumn border,[12] alongside the dahlia (first seen in Europe in the late eighteenth century), Chinese aster, hollyhock, Michaelmas daisy and the golden rod. Phillips records that more than thirty varieties were available in England, having

> escaped from the confinement of the conservatories of the curious, and as rapidly spread themselves over every part of our island, filling the casements of the cottagers and the parterres of the opulent with their autumnal beauties, that now vie with the Asters of their native land in splendour and variety of colour.[13]

The range of colour was in fact so notable that Phillips took the creators of early nomenclature to task for having assigned the name 'chrysos-anthum' to a flower that was no longer necessarily gold. Running through the possible permutations of petal shape, arrangement and colour, Phillips enthuses over 'changeable white, quilled white, tasselled white' and plain 'superb white'. Yellows ranged from buff to orange and flame, and reds from pale rose to rich crimson as well as the old purple and ruby or claret colour. This in an age when both port and claret were more frequent visitors to dining tables than now and the nuances of such colour descriptions would be more widely appreciated. Blue was sadly missing, but Phillips held out hope that a lilac shade, planted in some acidic soil such as bog or heath earth, might bring that desired shade into effect. Recommended not just for the flowerbed but also for the house, the chrysanthemum would bring colour long after most plants had faded away for the year – even, as Phillips mysteriously suggests, 'to those parts of the house where more delicate plants would not stand in flower'. Doused in the liquid from sewers, stables and outhouses to encourage fine and large blooms, and grown in large pots (a No. 38 was recommended), they were ideal for display, bringing colour to a dull afternoon tea table and flamboyance to an evening dinner party, although perhaps

Reds, maroons, yellow and whites predominated as chrysanthemum colours in the early 19th century.

a good wash might be needed before they decorated the dining room after their sojourn in sewer water.[14]

It was not just around the tea tables of the middle classes that tea and chrysanthemums combined. Sent to China as Assistant Inspector of Tea for the British East India Company in 1812, John Reeves (1774–1856) spent at least twenty years in his adopted country, returning to England only twice in that time and eventually rising to Chief Inspector; his son, also John, lived in China for thirty years. One of John Reeves's neighbours was John Livingstone (? – *c.* 1826), a surgeon for the Company, who had a particular interest in vegetables and other 'economic' plants, while another neighbour, Thomas Beale (*c.* 1775–1841), was a keen naturalist and gardener, noted for his hospitality and generosity as well as for being a speculator in opium. Their movements in mainland China were greatly restricted due to the particular regulations placed on foreigners, and so these amateur naturalists obtained their specimens of mammals, birds and fish from the market in Canton, while many of their plants came from the

Fa-tee Nurseries in that area. Here many choice specimens were grown for the local market, among them cultivars of camellia, peony and chrysanthemum.

Anxious to share such floral riches, including the numerous different chrysanthemum varieties, with their native England, Reeves and his fellow 'explorers' decided to embark the plants on one of the East India ships bound for the West. Even on a fast tea clipper this was a journey of several months, and a large proportion of plants would usually not survive the journey. Reeves, however, was a cautious character and took great trouble in preparing plants for shipping to

A multi-headed chrysanthemum plant from the John Reeves Collection of Botanical Drawings from Canton, China, collected between 1812 and 1831.

England, establishing them in pots long before the journey, and his success in this may be measured by his claim to have introduced some seventy varieties of chrysanthemum to England, including the cream/rosy-petalled and slightly nodding 'Drunken Lady', probably that referred by William Curtis as 'the Drunken Woman'. Reeves also commissioned a series of paintings from Chinese artists illustrating the flora and fauna of Canton, and in many cases it was these drawings (many now preserved in the Natural History Museum in London) that gave Western science the first glimpse of a Chinese species in all its glory. Perhaps less popular with gardeners is the prolific Muntjac deer (*Muntjac reevesii*) 'discovered' by his circle of naturalist friends and introduced to England along with the Reeves pheasant.

Abraham Hume (1749–1838) was from a considerably wealthier background than Reeves. A floriculturalist by interest and a baronet by birth, he was also a Fellow of the Royal Society, founding member of the Geological Society, Fellow of the Horticultural Society and (in his spare time from these pursuits) a politician. Florists are especially indebted to him for his introductions of Chinese peonies between 1798 and 1820 but, through his role in Indian and Chinese trading routes, he also sponsored the discovery and shipping to Europe of chrysanthemums. Many of these plants made their way to his family estate at Wormleybury in Hertfordshire, but many were also shared among the chrysanthemum lovers of the period, expanding the numbers of Chinese varieties available. Several members of the Hume family were involved in the East India Company trade to Canton, including Captain Alexander Hume (ship's captain for the company, d. 1800) and another Alexander, elder brother of Abraham Hume, who was also a director of the East India Company.[15] The online gardening resource www.helpmefind.com, which lists plants for sale, nurseries, events, and also plant introductions and historic nurseries, includes Wormleybury estate as having been a 'nursery' – so extensive were its connections. In an age when an association with the East India Company was about the only 'trade' a gentleman was allowed to engage in without losing his position in society, this modern classification of the historic family estate would have horrified the Hume family, although they might have been mollified by knowing that their contributions to plant introductions are still remembered.

Best known for his exploits stealing Chinese tea plants for the British Empire, the Scottish plant hunter Robert Fortune (1812– 1880) also added another twist to the tangled tale of chrysanthemum types. Born in Kelloe, Berwickshire, Fortune had worked at both the Royal Botanic Gardens Edinburgh and the Horticultural Society's garden at Chiswick in London before being sent out to China by the Society, supposedly to collect flowering plants. China had been reluc- tant to allow the British unhindered access to the floral and cultural wealth of the interior of the country and had, until 1842, attempted to restrict free-ranging merchants and plant hunters – hence the necessity for John Reeves to acquire plants from the Fa-tee Nurseries.

However, after the first (of several) Opium Wars of 1839–42 a treaty was imposed on China which allowed foreigners access via a series of ports where trade could be undertaken with anyone, rather than the existing Canton system. This not only made trade easier for Europeans, but made it more difficult for the Chinese to police the influx of foreigners, who might then slip into parts of the vast empire still theoretically forbidden. Robert Fortune was to be one of these. His shopping list of plants, provided by the Horticultural Society, included both ornamental and also economically 'useful' plants – hinting at the important role he was later to play in the economic sabotage of China by illegally collecting and exporting tea plants from China to India, the latter then part of the British Empire.

Fortune was also tasked with learning more about Chinese gar- dening and horticultural techniques, including examining the peaches growing in the gardens of the emperor. The quiet (some said sullen) disposition of Fortune and his knowledge of Mandarin, plus his enthusiasm for dressing in a Chinese manner, even growing a pigtail

overleaf: Small 'pompom' chrysanthemums were developed from the Chusan daisy discovered by Robert Fortune.

and shaving the rest of his hair, enabled him to pass as a (rather tall) local, and he was able to travel into areas forbidden to Europeans. Nevertheless, his travels were eventful, including shipwreck and attack by pirates, thieves and bandits as well as episodes of fever. During the three years of his first expedition he was rewarded with some of the most popular plants that still grace our flower borders, including Rosa Fortune's double yellow rose, the Japanese anemone, many varieties of the tree peony (long cultivated in north China), *Weigela rosea, Daphne fortunei, Jasminium nudiflorum, Skimmia japonica fortunei, Berberis japonica* and *Dicentra spectabilis*, besides various azaleas and, of course, chrysanthemums.

Arriving home in 1846, via Manila, Fortune introduced to England a seemingly undistinguished semi-double light brown chrysanthemum with small but numerous flower-heads. Found on the island of Chusan off the east coast of China, it was henceforth to be known as the Chusan daisy. Technically the property of the Horticultural Society, who had funded Fortune's three years of travels, propagated slips were sent out to the Society's members across Britain, but also to one Monsieur Lebois in Paris. Working in the more favourable climate of Paris, Lebois was able to get the plant to set seed and eventually raised numerous different cultivars, many of which naturally made their way back to England. These new varieties of chrysanthemum, or Chusan daisies, were given the common name of Pompom (or sometimes Pompon or Pompone) from their similarity to the adornment of the beret worn by French sailors, and for many years were claimed to be the only chrysanthemum that would reliably flower early enough for outdoor cultivation.

This delightful history, encompassing the common habiliments of both China and France, and chrysanthemums with a preference for Continental climates, is only slightly marred by the appearance of small multi-petalled varieties of chrysanthemum in the *Transactions of the Horticultural Society* of 1821 and again in 1826 in articles by Joseph Sabine which bear a singular resemblance to the Pompom (or Pompon) of Fortune. The resemblance may be explained by the presence in China in the 1820s of an earlier plant hunter called Mr Parks, who was also employed by the Horticultural Society and was honoured with the naming of the suspiciously daisy-sounding 'Parks's Small Yellow'. By 1850 there were numerous Chusan daisy cultivars and the *Gardeners' Magazine of Botany* of that year presented four sorts as a colour plate. It was presumably the later (re-)introduction to which the famous cookery and household writer Mrs Beeton was referring when she commented in the mid-nineteenth century that 'The introduction of this little favourite has tended in no small degree to resuscitate the cultivation of the chrysanthemum.'[16] Robert Fortune also recorded seeing in China the larger flowering chrysanthemums of the 'sinensis' type, by then well known in Britain and France, describing 'banks of gorgeous blooms [that] are illuminated at night with lanterns, and even gigantic effigies are made up entirely of their lovely flowers'.[17]

After that initial expedition, and a pause in which he wrote up his adventures in the rather all-encompassing book *Three Years' Wanderings in the Northern Provinces of China, including a visit to the tea, silk, and cotton countries, with an account of the agriculture and horticulture of the Chinese*, Fortune set off again on behalf of the East India Company to collect plants and seeds of the tea plant. In 1851 he successfully introduced 2,000 plants and 17,000 sprouting seeds of tea into the northwestern provinces of India, as described in *A Journey to the Tea Countries of China* (1852), by which time one might have imagined that any officials in China responsible for the control of trade and economy would have banned him from the country immediately. However, he returned in 1857 to collect more tea shrubs and other plants, this time on behalf of the U.S. Patent Office, as well as visiting rice-paper regions of Taiwan and the silkworm regions of China. It appears to be during these latter trips that Fortune encountered, and predictably 'collected', some Japanese types of chrysanthemum that, after being featured in *Curtis's Botanical Magazine* in 1863, were largely to be developed by French and Guernsey growers who could predictably set their seed.

Fortune himself appears to have settled down after a life of touring the economic and plant wealth of China and Japan, engaging for a while in farming in his home country of Scotland. Although rice and peaches do not grow well in Scotland, there is a modern and burgeoning tea industry there thanks to the inspiration of Robert Fortune. Established in 2010 by entrepreneur Tam O'Braan, the tea farm at Dalreoch boasts 14,000 tea plants on formerly sheep-grazed slopes. This is just part of an industry that now spreads from the island of Mull to the Scottish lowlands, linked by a dedicated Scottish tea-growers' association; tea plants raised here are high in antioxidants and include a premium 'white tea', among others.[18] In his travels Fortune also noted that the Chinese make a drink from the flowers of the chrysanthemum, which he said was regarded as an *elixir vitae* very much in the way that the British regard tea. Indeed he might have saved himself a lot of time and effort smuggling tea plants if he could only have persuaded the English to drink chrysanthemum tea instead.

Alongside the influx of chrysanthemums directly imported from China by Fortune were new cultivars being raised by men such as John Salter (1798–1874), to whom Fortune had entrusted some of his Chusan daisies. Salter had long had an interest in chrysanthemums, and, basing himself in France, had been able to produce a number of seedlings of both Chusan and non-Chusan types, which he named after French heroes and sites and then advertised in the English press. In 1841 he 'begged to inform' friends and possible customers that he had seedlings of 'Princess Marie', 'Napoleon', 'Pygmalion', 'Gouvion St Cyr' and 'Reine Murat'.[19] In 1847 he introduced what were to be his most famous varieties, 'Annie Salter' (named after his daughter) and the patriotic 'Queen of England', both bred at Versailles and both still listed in the National Chrysanthemum Society Register more than 110 years later.

After the French *coup d'état* of 1848, John Salter was forced to return to England, where he continued to breed chrysanthemums at his nursery in Hammersmith, London, which he rather confusingly

Thomas Allom, 'The Culture and Preparation of Tea', from George Newenham
Wright, *China in a Series of Views* (1843).

named the Versailles Nursery. His most famous flower, the 'Queen
of England', provided Salter with a series of 'sports' or spontaneous
changes uncontrolled or unexpected by the nurseryman. One of
these he named 'Empress of India' (a primrose colour) while another
was called 'Versailles Defiance'. In 1840 Salter claimed to have
between three hundred and four hundred distinctly different kinds
of chrysanthemum, leading the way in what was to be the popular
hardy chrysanthemum market. Over the next twenty years his annual
display became, in the words of the *Gardener's Magazine* of 1868,

> an established floral tradition of the metropolis, for it is a
> show of no mean order. Year by year it becomes more exten-
> sive, and at the same time more varied in its details. No
> description we can give will do due justice to this admirable
> winter-garden, when seen about the second week in Novem-
> ber, just as autumn is merging into winter; and when 'The
> flush of the landscape is o'er, The brown leaves are shed on
> the way.'[20]

The 'show' was in fact the nursery itself rather than a show in the
term we might mean, that is with numerous societies and individuals

John Salter's
Chrysanthemum
'Versailles Defiance',
from *The Garden
Companion and Florists'
Guide* (1852).

competing against each other – although that was soon to come.[21] In 1865 John Salter published *The Chrysanthemum: Its History and Culture*, which caused the reviewer for the *Gardeners' Chronicle (and Agricultural Gazette)* to opine 'When Mr Salter discourses on Chrysanthemums it is the Oracle that speaks.'

However, Salter's claim to fame comes not just from his individual specimens but from the techniques he used and the resulting variation they produced, and it was that which attracted the attention of the evolutionary scientist Charles Darwin. Darwin's seminal work *On the Origin of Species by Means of Natural Selection* was published in 1859 and is now his most famous, but Darwin regarded it as merely an abstract of his theories and immediately began work on a new, more detailed, book entitled *The Variation of Animals and Plants under Domestication*. During the research for this Darwin noted that he 'applied to two great authorities on the subject [of bud variation], namely, to Mr Rivers with respect to fruit-trees, and to Mr Salter with respect to flowers'.[22]

Darwin exchanged ideas with John Salter about the nature and fixity of variations in botany and the best conditions for maintaining and altering them, the very thing that Salter was attempting to achieve with his chrysanthemums. Darwin was fascinated that Salter mimicked nature in using the most appropriate buds or stock to refine and fix new varieties. This active selection of plant material was especially important for chrysanthemums, which often did not set seed in England or breed true. It was a sort of proactive, interventionist version of the survival of the fittest and an experimental 'proof' of Darwin's ideas, so that many of John Salter's observations found their way into Darwin's new book when it was published in 1868.[23] Salter himself published a small monograph, *The Chrysanthemum: Its History and Culture*, in 1865, with hand-coloured plates by James Andrews and a complete list of chrysanthemum cultivars available, but somehow

By the end of the 19th century the bizarre shapes of the anemone and spider had joined the incurve and reflex chrysanthemum.

A modern spider or 'Fuji' form of chrysanthemum.

it never attained the notoriety of Darwin's more famous work, although its rarity puts a high price on copies nowadays.[24]

Back with the tea-smuggling Robert Fortune: in 1862 Fortune introduced a further seven varieties of 'Japanese' chrysanthemum into England which were to revolutionize the large-flowered chrysanthemum to the same extent that the Chusan had the small-flowered hardy plants. These new Japanese forms varied from those described as 'fantastic forms', such as the Dragons (or less mythically 'anemone types'), to fringed forms and those which had incurved or reflexed petals or resembled camellias. These new arrivals had much stronger stems and were of better growing habit than the old small incurves (which were often very tall with thin stems and had a tendency to break in the vase, giving the impression of long-legged crane-flies), and their ability to stand tall despite the heaviest weight of flower-head made these chrysanthemums ideal for the show table. One remarked upon by the nurseryman Salter, which had a 'long narrow hair-like fringe', had unfortunately not reached Europe alive, and one can sense in Salter's writings his sad longing for this missing child among the other bizarres.

It was a slow beginning for the chrysanthemum, as Arthur Herrington recounted in his seminal work on *The Chrysanthemum: Its Culture for Professional Growers and Amateurs. A Practical Treatise on Its Propagation, Cultivation, Training, Raising for Exhibition and Market, Hybridising, Origin and History* (1923): 'So singular were these in shape and colour from all reputed standards of perfection at the time, that they barely escaped total neglect, and consequent extinction.'[25] However, these were the strains that would eventually become the most fashionable, in part due to their very singularity. By the end of the nineteenth century variations in the fancy chrysanthemum resulted in numer-ous show classes, including the pompom, the incurved, the recurved, the ostrich plume and the spiders, spoons and quills or when all else failed 'the Irregular': all part of the complex, almost mystical, terminology.[26]

three

Gathering the Harvest in Societies and Shows

With such a range of colours and shapes, and the lure of being able to develop even more, it was not long before the chrysanthemum came to the attention of the flower fanciers who were generally known into the nineteenth century as 'florists'. Unlike the modern meaning of someone who will sell you a flower or deliver a whole bouquet, 'florists' and florists' societies were then dedicated to the raising and showing of a limited number of flower types. In the eighteenth century, when the societies originated, these types were restricted to the auricula, carnation, polyanthus, ranunculus and tulip; in the late eighteenth century they were joined by the pink. Less specialized shows might also permit classes for what we now regard as humble cottage garden flowers such as the antirrhinum, petunia and (later on) the calceolaria and pelargonium.[1]

By the time the chrysanthemum had become popular, however, this range of florists' flowers had been expanded to include the anemone, hollyhock (surely a difficult flower to bring to a show table), pansy, picotee and latterly the dahlia, such that the inclusion of its autumnal cousin the chrysanthemum was almost inevitable. Nevertheless, in the early decades of the nineteenth century there was some reluctance to welcome the foreign chrysanthemum to the European florists' table. Although the dahlia had been welcomed with open arms in the eighteenth century 'with all its splendid varieties of colour and form', according to Joseph Harrison of the

Floricultural Cabinet and Florist's Magazine in 1833, the chrysanthemum for some reason languished out in the cold.[2] A. H. Howarth, writing in John Claudius Loudon's *Gardener's Magazine* in April 1833, noted that

> Chinese chrysanthemums have not hitherto ranked with the true flowers of the florist because, however well formed, in many of the varieties, they are all, save the Gold-bordered Red, of self or uniform colours: and the florist requires yet another colour or colours to be distinctly depicted upon the first of ground colour of every petal to constitute his favourite flakes, bizarres and picotees.[3]

In the same article Howarth attempted a list of possible classes for chrysanthemums, should their colours ever increase, based on shape and including Ranunculus-flowered, Incurved Ranunculus-flowered, China Aster-flowered, Marigold-flowered, Tassel-flowered and Half-double Tassel-flowered,[4] a selection which you would have thought would keep any florist content. But it was the arrival of the 'Gold-bordered Red' which was to be the saving grace, permitting the attempted breeding of stripes so favoured by florists in all things floral.

Development of flower type and size had already been happening away from the florists' show bench and the pursuit of the stripe, so that by 1825 there were already 48 varieties of chrysanthemum on show in the Horticultural Society grounds in London. Some of these were taken to France by Louis Noisette, better known now for his work on the development of Noisette roses. In 1830 (other sources say 1832) a Mr Isaac Wheeler of Magdalen College Oxford was awarded the silver Banksian Medal of the Horticultural Society for raising seedlings of a large flowered variety of chrysanthemum. In 1831 a George Harrison of Downham in Norfolk protected late plant-ings under glass with stunning returns for seeds and the prospect of raising new cultivars from seedlings rather than cuttings – thus allow-ing greater variation. A fellow resident of Downham, John Freestone

This medal from the National Chrysanthemum Society depicts the types of chrysanthemum which could be entered in the various show classes.

of Watlington Hall, has also been claimed as the first man to raise chrysanthemums from seed in the UK, possibly using the same glass methods to create nine new varieties, and one can only hope the two worked in a spirit of neighbourliness and not rivalry.

Anxious to share these wonders beyond the confines of Downham, George Harrison is supposed to have been the instigator of the first-ever chrysanthemum show, held in Norwich in 1843.[5] The first chrysanthemum society was formed just three years later in 1846 (the very same year that Robert Fortune returned from his first expedition to China) as the Stoke Newington Florists' Society for the Cultivation and Exhibition of the Chrysanthemum (later to become the Borough of Hackney Chrysanthemum Society and later still the National Chrysanthemum Society). There must have been some chrysanthemums exhibited in more general shows in Stoke Newington prior to the formation of the Society itself, as F. W. Burbidge's 1884 history of the chrysanthemum tells us that a 'Mr Short and a Mr Freestone, about the year 1835, showed "Nonpareil" and "Norfolk Hero" at the first public Chrysanthemum show for cut blooms at Stoke Newington.'⁶ From its name, 'Norfolk Hero' was presumably one of Mr Freestone's own cultivars.

Stoke Newington, then a village on the north edge of London, may seem an unlikely place for the chrysanthemum to strike out, but not only had many of Robert Fortune's Chinese introductions found their way to the nursery of Samuel Brookes in Stoke Newington, but the parish also housed one of the foremost garden writers of the period, James Shirley Hibberd (1825–1890). Hibberd was both a guru and a maverick in the Victorian gardening world. Managing to combine a confidently aspirational middle-class approach, so typical of his period, with a quirky personal life that encompassed an early devotion to vegetarianism, a love of wildlife and parrots and a passion for bees (which he suggested could be kept inside the house for their greater comfort), he also experimented with opium and cannabis and after the death of his first wife married his cook.

Hibberd kept up what might best be described as a 'lively' correspondence with many of the other garden writers of the day, decrying much of their output and views, and published his own advice to amateur gardeners and homemakers in a stream of works with titles calculated to lure the suburban masses with hopes of self-improvement, carefully combined with nostalgia for the rural past. The patently urbanite *The Town Garden* (1855) was followed by the contrasting *Brambles and Bay Leaves: Essays on the Homely and the Beautiful* in the same year, before he got into his publishing stride with what would be his best-selling work, *Rustic Adornments for Homes of Taste* (1856). Seeing a willing market, his publishers encouraged him to set up a monthly magazine for amateur gardeners, entitled *The Floral World and Garden Guide*, which covered all aspects of gardening.

Hibberd moved so frequently (although always within London) that it is surprising that he had any time to establish a garden. Born in Mile End Old Town, both of his parents had died by the time he was in his mid-twenties. His marriage to Sarah Voyer resulted in a move to a house in Pentonville, followed a few years later by a house in Tottenham. In 1856 he was still living in Tottenham, but within two years took a house in Lordship Terrace, Stoke Newington (close to the nursery of Samuel Brookes). From Stoke Newington a series of works issued which made him one of the most influential garden writers of the Victorian period. In 1862 he took over the *Gardener's Weekly Magazine*, an ailing publication, which he relaunched in 1865 as the *Gardeners' Magazine* (later cunningly changing the position of the apostrophe to differentiate it from the earlier *Gardener's Magazine*). This became a serious rival to the well-established periodicals the *Gardeners' Chronicle* and the *Cottage Gardener* and put him in the forefront of horticultural publishing.

From 1863 onwards Hibberd produced titles on every aspect of gardening, including *Profitable Gardening*, *The Rose Book*, *The Fern Garden*, *The Amateur's Flower Garden*, *The Amateur's Greenhouse and Conservatory* and *The Amateur's Kitchen Garden*, and was the first person to make a study of ivy with his monograph *The Ivy*, followed by a book about wild flowers, *Field Flowers*. Two series of his works, *New and Rare Beautiful-leaved Plants* and *Familiar Garden Flowers*, were produced with coloured plates (an expensive outlay at this date). In 1884 Hibberd started another magazine, *Amateur Gardening*, which survives today. He also took time to write *Home Culture of the Watercress*, for which he was awarded a gold medal by the Royal Horticultural Society. In fact, the one topic on which Hibberd does not seem to have published a book was the chrysanthemum. He did, however, include chrysanthemums in his very popular work *The Amateur's Flower Garden* (1871), promoting its charms to all amateur gardeners by calling it a 'grand autumnal flower that meets with scant attention from the thousands of amateurs whose necessities and conveniences it appears exactly adapted to'.

By the late nineteenth century, the gardens of the working and middle classes in London and other large conurbations were suffering from the effects of smog and pollution – a combination of acids and blanketing soots that resulted in grey and grimy gardens. The chrysanthemum, suggested Hibberd, would bring a golden cheer to these otherwise dull gardens at the worst time of year, when mists and the first coal fires of the season brought down the heavy pea soupers; and it was not just the garden that the chrysanthemums would enliven but the gardeners themselves. Whether it was the smog, or the thought of bleak winter putting a stop to their enjoyments, autumn suicide rates in the cities were, Hibberd believed, worryingly high among gardeners as well as the general populace and he advocated the chrysanthemum as the cure for these ills. Armed with statistics collected by the town authorities, Hibberd proposed that as

> chrysanthemum growing became a metropolitan garden fashion – perhaps a mania, and a very good one . . . it appears that from the date of the dethronement of Louis Philippe in 1848 and the first multiplication of chrysanthemum societies, November suicides began to decrease in number, so that now every well-intentioned city, town and village has its annual show, the month of November is found to be less characterized by suicides than any month in all the year.[7]

The golden flowers shone out, he said, despite the depressive gloom of the autumn afternoons, and in support of his theory he argued that more money was taken at chrysanthemum shows in the one hour after 6 p.m. than at any other time of day.[8] Despite this heartening news on the effect of the chrysanthemum on a depressed populace, Hibberd notes that 'rarely [is] a border liberally furnished with the best varieties', although gardens of florists were an exception.

Hibberd's cultivation advice, designed to encourage the plants' proliferation in pursuit of the general increase of the population's happiness, may have shocked some of the more dedicated growers. On the subject of the hardier varieties, for example, he notes that all that is required is to 'Plant in good soil and keep the plants securely staked from the first' – and that's it. As he says, all you need to know in thirteen words, although he does go on to mention manures, and reduction of shoots and occasionally pegging down – but these things he declares are 'supplementary rather than necessary'. 'Stopping out' is, he claimed, never necessary for the border plant, releasing gardeners from this tedious task to address the hundreds of others that claim their attention. However, with a tendency for the plants to collapse at the first frosts, those with restricted or no access to glasshouses had to take extreme measures to protect their November 'sunshine'.

Other protective measures recommended in the 1860s included covering the plants with temporary frames and inserting rush lights to burn through the night, a practice one would have thought would be very likely to result in a conflagration of not only the flowerbeds but of adjoining small houses. More safety-conscious individuals could use a zinc pipe and a small boiler to heat the frames with an oil lamp.[9] The arrival of miniature varieties of chrysanthemums in the late nineteenth century meant that the flowers could be squeezed into the very smallest of garden or even be incorporated into the popular 'bedding' systems which during summer held bright salvias, petunias and pelargoniums.[10]

Hibberd believed that the sunny yellows of the chrysanthemum could lift the autumn spirits of Londoners.

Staking, debudding, pegging down and all manner of care from the anxious gardener were usually recommended to chrysanthemum growers.

Hibberd was an active member of the Stoke Newington Chrysanthemum Society and was its president in 1860. After moving again (to Muswell Hill) he continued to promote the chrysanthemum, which included attending national chrysanthemum conferences, one in 1889 and then in 1890, the year of his death. It was perhaps because of such connections that he was able to list in *The Amateur's Flower Garden* the 'Best One Hundred Chrysanthemums', divided into Incurved, Reflexed, Large Anemones, Pompones (*sic*) and Japanese, as they would have been termed for the show bench. The list includes a sprinkling of French names (especially among the 'Pompones') as well as the stalwart English varieties, some still carrying the names of the nurserymen so important in their history such as John Salter (Incurved) and James Salter (Japanese).

As with all show flowers at this time, many cultivars had honorific namings drawing on members of the aristocracy, who probably paid little heed to the honour done to them. 'Lady Hardinge', 'Lady Slade', 'Lord Derby', 'Princess Beatrice' (all incurves) alongside 'Prince Albert' (reflex) and the large anemone cultivars 'Mrs Pethers', 'Lady Margaret', 'Princess Marguerite' and 'Queen Margaret'. Only Japanese varieties had any hint of the Asiatic origins of the chrysanthemum, with 'Emperor of China', 'Nagasaki Violet' (did this have a hint of the rare blue?), 'Red Dragon' and 'The Mikado', alongside the rather more puzzling names of 'The Sultan', 'Wizard' and the rather wonderful 'Prince Satsuma', the last presumably an orange variety.

By the end of the nineteenth century, the number of types of flower-head on the fancy chrysanthemum had increased even beyond the vocabulary of the flower fancier and competitive classes were defined both by the flowering time and form of the flower-head.[11] Descriptions were increasingly poetic if not hyperbolic. The advertisement for the 'New White Ostrich Plume "Mrs Alpheus Hardy"', referred to its

> immense size, broad petals incurved, the surface being downy, like loose-piled plush. The entire flower seems frosted with glittering white. Its unique character consists in its fine, downy appearance.

Apparently the flower was only surpassed by the even more plume-like 'Mrs Anna Manda', which must have been a blow to Mrs Alpheus Hardy – whoever she was.

Despite dying in Kew (rather appropriately for a garden writer), Hibberd was buried in Abney Park Cemetery in Stoke Newington, the home of the chrysanthemum. Unsurprisingly, the cause of death was over-work, or as the *Gardeners' Chronicle* described it, he was a 'victim of his own zeal'.

Another man who combined a zealous approach to gardening and an adoration for the chrysanthemum was Samuel Broome

(1805–1870). Broome was the head gardener of the Great Garden at London's Inner Temple for 38 years. Taking up his post in 1842, he had been gardener at the Inner Temple just four years before the arrival of the hardier Pompom chrysanthemums that were to transform the gardens of the capital. Despite the pollution from the gasworks next door at Bridewell and from the factories on the Surrey bank of the river, the hardy little chrysanthemum thrived in the Inner Temple Garden.

In 1858 Broome published a book aimed at encouraging more town gardeners to adopt the chrysanthemum, entitling it *Culture of the Chrysanthemum, as Practised in the Temple Gardens; To which is added a list of plants suited to the atmosphere of London and other large towns, with hints for their management.* Despite its lengthy title, the work became so popular that it reached eighteen editions, the last coming out in 1893: a testimony to both Broome's authority and the impact of smog on city gardeners. Each edition carried recommendations for new varieties and cultivars, which enables chrysanthemum historians to track the comings (and goings), successes (and failures) over the decades between those first and last editions.

Next door at the Middle Temple, the head gardener Joseph Dale also bred and exhibited chrysanthemums, and in 1867 the two gardeners, Dale and Broome, came together to publish a joint edition of the chrysanthemum book, whose title, referring as it did to the 'Temple Gardens', was fortunately inclusive enough not to need changing. During the 1860s, in his *Floral World and Garden Guides*, Shirley Hibberd commented very favourably each year on the free displays for the public that were offered by both the gardens and gardeners at the Temple Gardens. Comparisons were inevitably made between the respective displays of Broome and Dale, although allowances were made for the 'more sheltered position' from the frosts and high winds that favoured the smaller more manageable Middle Temple Garden. Back at the Inner Temple, thanks to the work of Samuel Broome, the gardens were thriving. *London: What to See and How to See It* reported in 1862 that:

Chrysanthemum Show in the Temple Gardens.

The garden is laid out and kept in good order. It is of con-
siderable extent, chiefly covered by greensward surrounded
on three sides with beds of flowers and has a gravelled walk
or terrace on the bank of the river commanding fine views
. . . During the months of October and November these
gardens are made radiant with a gay profusion of chrysanthemums by the gardener Mr Broome who has rendered
the Temple Gardens as one of the most attractive shows of
the Seasons, and the gardens are then freely open to the
public.[12]

In his *Walks and Talks about London* (1865), John Timbs also described Broome's gardens and their success with the public, remarking that

> in the flower-beds next to the main walk he [Broome] managed to secure four successive crops of flowers – the pompons were especially gaudy and beautiful; but his chief triumph was the chrysanthemums of the northern border. Two hundred families enjoy these gardens throughout the year, and about 10,000 of the outer world, chiefly children, who are always in search of the lost Eden, come here annually. The flowers and trees are rarely injured, thanks to the much-abused London public.[13]

In 1861, Broome wrote to the editor of the *Penny Illustrated Paper*:

> the working classes are getting passionately fond of flowers and those among them who enjoy the advantage of a sunny spot of ground out of town cultivate them in their leisure hours on summer evenings as an amusement. They form themselves into little societies. They exhibit their productions in friendly rivalry with one another and those who are successful go away highly delighted with their prizes.[14]

Broome's reputation spread beyond the precincts of the Inner Temple and earned him a place as honoured guest at the first annual dinner of the Tower Hamlets Chrysanthemum Society, held on 5 December 1859 at the Eagle Tavern in Mile End. The chairman, George Glenny, declared that 'floriculture had never made such progress among the people as within the last eighteen months.' He quoted from Samuel Broome, as 'the floral oracle of the working classes', and repeated Broome's claim that 'the chrysanthemum was the only flower the working classes could successfully cultivate without an expense beyond his means.'[15]

Broome's fame was to extend much further than his beloved London. In 1883 John Thorpe, the 'father of the chrysanthemum' in America, looked back upon his own success and explained that it was due to Samuel Broome: he recalled his childhood in London and climbing up on 'Old Sam' Broome's knee, where he was told all about chrysanthemums, how they were such a lovely and neglected flower and how they were destined to become popular. One day, he said, 'Sam' sent him fifty flowers and a copy of his book, which he would never part with, 'not even for $1,000', a gift which made him determined to make the chrysanthemum the most popular autumn flower in America. By the time of Thorpe's reminiscences, Samuel Broome had been dead for thirteen years, although his influence has lasted to the modern day, both at the Inner Temple Garden and among chrysanthemum showers and breeders of all classes. He was buried at Nunhead Cemetery (London Borough of Southwark), and friends erected an obelisk-style monument to his memory with his name, dates and a chrysanthemum engraved upon it. A brief notice of his death read:

> Samuel Broome, for forty years gardener to the Honourable Society of the Inner Temple, whose annual Chrysanthemum Show was one of the sights of London, and who, in their culture, gave such valuable testimony to the effects of Lord Palmerston's Smoke Act, is dead, at a ripe old age. He lived respected, and he died happy.[16]

A lengthier appreciation of his skills was published in the *Gardeners' Chronicle* (January 1870), which included this from his old friend Dale of the Middle Temple Garden: Broome was 'a genial, warm-hearted, persevering man, he was alike respected by rich and poor, and earned himself the reputation of being a true philanthropist. Not that he was rich as the word goes in this worlds [*sic*] goods, but he was ever ready to give valuable counsel and assistance to the humbler classes' – most especially, as Dale goes on to say, in the matter of chrysanthemum growing.[17]

A more poetic notice in the periodical *Punch* combined a eulogy for Broome with a sly dig at the legal profession:

Poor old Broome, art thou gone! and shall we hear
Thy annual Jubilate never more,
O'er the Chrysanthemums that were so dear
Unto thy honest heart, as, year by year,
They decked the Temple Garden's swarded floor!
. . . the gleam
Of the Chrysanthemums thou didst adore –
Never was simple man more glad than thou,
Never were gentler pride and joy than thine –
Pleased to see pleased crowds round thy Pompons bow,
Children, maids, barristers of parchment brow,
Who rarely noticed sun's or blossom's shine.
Along Thames' bank thy blooms stood brave and bold,
The brighter for the brick and mortar round:
And if thy flowers were flowers of gold,
So innocent none grew from Temple mould,
None so enriched, yet cumbered not, the ground.[18]

In recognition of the great chrysanthemum shows of Broome and Dale, the then new 'Royal Courts of Justice Restaurant' at 222 the Strand (until recently a Lloyds Bank) was decorated with Royal Doulton tiles depicting some of the five hundred varieties of chrysanthemums exhibited at the 1882 show, including a dusky pink one called 'Inner Temple'.[19]

Back in Stoke Newington, where it had all begun, early chrysanthemum society meetings were usually held at public houses, including most frequently the Amwell Arms and the Rochester Castle. Meeting in public houses was common among florists' societies of the eighteenth and early nineteenth centuries and consuming drink was part of the contract between society and publican. Back rooms were set aside for the purpose of showing and in some instances empty beer

bottles were used to display the flower-heads: a tradition anathema to Hibberd, who was teetotal.[20] The competition at Stoke Newington was usually for twelve blooms, although there was an increasing number of classes for the burgeoning varieties. A report of the 1852 show refers to blooms 15 centimetres (6 in.) across, demonstrating the diligence with which early growers tended to their plants, although there was general agreement in the 1850s that the finest was 'Queen of England', one of Salter's cultivars.

In 1874 the society's name was changed to the Stoke Newington and Hackney Chrysanthemum Society, perhaps reflecting the influence of Hibberd on the proceedings, and three years later, in 1877, the shows (three a year) were being held at the Royal Aquarium with a grant from the Aquarium Company. An aquarium seems an odd location for a flower show, but in addition to the aquatic displays, the venue had a conveniently large exhibition space for the ever-expanding blooms, as by this time vases of 48 heads were often shown. In 1884 the society changed its name again, this time expanding its remit from a small area of north London to become the National Chrysanthemum Society and also introducing a subcommittee to deal with the influx of new varieties. From now on society meetings were frequently held at the Anderton Hotel in Fleet Street rather than the old

In the 19th century the Royal Aquarium was the venue for the National Chrysanthemum Society shows.

ROYAL AQUARIUM

WESTMINSTER.

MID-WINTER

FLOWER SHOW

OF THE NATIONAL

CHRYSANTHEMUM

SOCIE TY.

Wednesday and Thursday,
JANUARY 11th and 12th, 1888,
**Chrysanthemums, Primulas, Cyclamen
&c.**
Schedules, &c., of WILLIAM HOLMES, Frampton Park Nurseries, Hackney.

Admission as usual One Shilling.

King Bros., Printers, Lymington.

haunts in north London pubs, and from 1903 until 1914 society exhibitions were transferred to the Crystal Palace, until it was commandeered by the army during the war. The National Chrysanthemum Society still holds the archive for these years, from which comes the following flavour of the work of the society at the turn of the century:

a visit made to Mr Percy Cragg's nursery in 1911. 'It was exceedingly kind and thoughtful of this firm to anticipate the comfort of those forming the party, as they did by the provision of ample accommodation in the way of horses and conveyances to make the visit more pleasurable and less of a tax on the members. The party had been on the move

Tiles commemorating the proximity of the Inner Temple Garden to what was the nearby Lloyds Bank.

The 1915 Finsbury Park Show, close to the original Stoke Newington 'headquarters' of the chrysanthemum.

for some hours, and darkness came upon the scene somewhat unexpectedly. However, the members of the firm had thought of creature comforts, and at the end of a large glass structure the good things in the way of hospitality had been provided in abundance, and it is unnecessary to add, the members of the party did ample justice to them.'[21]

Away from Stoke Newington and Hackney, the number of local chrysanthemum societies in London increased through the decades of the nineteenth century, including societies in Bermondsey, Kennington and Camden Town. The first annual dinner of the Tower Hamlets Chrysanthemum Society took place on 5 December 1859 at the Eagle Tavern in Mile End, an occasion on which the chairman, George Glenny, noted the vital role played by Samuel Broome in the promotion of the chrysanthemum and working-class horticulture generally. Even among more rural village or district horticultural and flower societies, the advent of the dahlia and the chrysanthemum onto the showing stage (or into the tent) led to the increase in the all-important 'shows' from twice a year to three times a year to account for these late bloomers.

As more societies sprang up so too did competition between them for everything from members to show dates. The Tower Hamlets Chrysanthemum Society Show was held annually in November, but in 1863 (under George Glenny) it was expanded to occupy three days. This meant that it overlapped with the first Great Chrysanthemum Show held at the Agricultural Halls in Islington. One member, eager to sweep the board at not just one show but both, removed his prize-winning chrysanthemums from the Tower Hamlets show before its conclusion, to place them in the Great Chrysanthemum Show, where they again won first prize. George Glenny insisted that this was against the rules of the Tower Hamlets Society, while others merely suggested that it showed great credit to the Society that their member could win at the Great Chrysanthemum Show as well the local one. The debate dragged on, becoming more and more acrimonious, until the following year, when the East Tower Hamlets Society and the Tower Hamlets Society staged a show on the same dates (in August, so presumably an early chrysanthemum type). Glenny was incensed and described the East Tower Hamlets Society as being comprised of 'scavengers who have scraped together the refuse of chrysanthemum societies' and 'men of incapacity and of miserably lower grade of intellect who can neither write a sentence in plain English nor spell the most common word'. Whether the latter was aimed at the East Tower Hamlets Society chairman (William Eickhoff) or the working-class men that made up the Society's members is uncertain, although one suspects that Glenny succeeded in upsetting both. He had a knack for annoying people with his often 'forthright' opinions on all things horticultural.

four
In Peace and in War

❦

Once in a while, the hard work and dedication of any horticulturalist or flower fancier is put to shame by Dame Luck and a mysterious 'sport' or spontaneous hybrid will revolutionize a plant that has been bred into all sorts of shapes and colours or desirable qualities over centuries, but previously never quite managed the promise that chance bestows upon it. Such was the case with the Rubellums group of chrysanthemum, which appeared as if by magic in a Welsh garden. Now often referred to as an 'old reliable' or a 'traditional cottage garden gem', the *Chrysanthemum x rubellum* is in fact of relatively recent birth, having been developed from the original sport from 1938 onwards by the nurseryman Amos Perry (about whom, more below).

Similar to the 'Korean' chrysanthemums, which are also multi-flowered garden chrysanthemums (in fact, hybridized in America), the *Chrysanthemum x rubellum* is that magical combination of a multi-flowered chrysanthemum in a wide variety of colours that is actually hardy in the United Kingdom, or at least most of it. In common with its native land of Wales, the actual birth of the Rubellums is some-what shrouded in mist. As we have seen, the plant hunter Robert Fortune is said to have brought back the first of these from China in 1846, under the name the Chusan daisy, and the 'rubellum type' was well known by the 1880s, being championed by the irascible 'Father of the English Flower Garden' William Robinson, at his garden at Gravetye Manor (Sussex). Robinson was one of the most influential garden writers and designers of the late nineteenth and early twentieth centuries. His favourite chrysanthemum, named 'Emperor of China', started out as soft pink and became darker as the temperatures dropped and the nights drew in. In a rather un-emperor-like way it needed good supporting and staking as it reached over a metre high.

The Rubellum types were widely grown and admired for their relative hardiness. However, the *Chrysanthemum* x *rubellum*s all originate from the wonderfully named 'Happy Valley Gardens' in Llandudno, where a plant was spotted by a diligent gardener as an 'odd one out' and referred to Kew's Royal Botanic Gardens for identification and, if necessary, naming. Kew botanist John Sealy thought that it was most like *Chrysanthemum zawadskii* var. *sibiricum*, but not quite enough like it to be the same species, and so it was awarded a new species name of *Chrysanthemum* x *rubellum*. In fact, advances in botanical science now suggest that he was wrong, and that the 'odd one out' was

The ostrich plume chrysanthemum was one of the new 'Bizarres' of the late 19th century in Europe and the USA.

probably not a new species and should have been named *Chrysanthemum zawadskii* var. *sibiricum robustrum*. Although if it had been so-named one can imagine it would not perhaps have hit the heights of popularity that the rather simpler *Chrysanthemum rubellum* did, as simply ordering it would have taken an age and involved linguistic challenges many might have decided simply to avoid.

The Happy Valley Gardens shared the new plant with several chrysanthemum breeders who used it to produce new hybrids that retained the hardiness of the original plant but improved on its colours and shape. Among these was the breeder Amos Perry, who produced one of the first dwarf Rubellums, 'Clara Curtis', a handy development for those who garden in locations where autumn winds can reach gale force, battering down any taller plants. Amos Perry (1871–1953), who was so fundamental to the development of the hardy garden 'mum', was one in a long line of Perry nurserymen. His great-grandfather had worked at the famous plant nursery owned by the Veitch family in Exeter, themselves great importers of plants from China and Japan and one-time sponsors of the plant hunter Ernest 'Chinese' Wilson. Perry's grandfather had been a rose-grower at the Ware company nursery in Tottenham. His father, also Amos Perry, had originally veered away from what appears to have been the Perry fate to become a nurseryman, and instead started his working life as an apprentice schoolteacher, but failing health led to a recommendation to go abroad, and not being in a position to do this he did the next best thing, which was to follow his forebears into the nurseries. At first Amos senior worked in the plant nurseries of Messrs Wingfield in Gloucestershire and then perhaps inevitably joined his own father at the firm of Messrs T. S. Ware, where he stayed for 25 years, eventually becoming a partner in what was then Messrs Ware, Fells and Perry.

The Perry name was thus linked inextricably with the world of plants and in particular the world of hardy plants. Out of fashion in the late Victorian period, when brightly coloured annual bedding plants reigned supreme, Amos senior nevertheless started to specialize in what are now regarded as the 'old-fashioned' stalwarts of the flower border, including echinacea, phlox, achillea, iris and of course the hardier garden chrysanthemums. Moving to start his own nurseries at Winchmore Hill, and then at Enfield, his success was bolstered by changing fashions with the publication of William Robinson's books *The English Flower Garden* (1883) and *The Wild Garden* (1870). *Achillea ptarmica* 'Perry's White', *Aster amellus* 'Perry's Favourite' and *Anchusa italica* 'Perry's' all come from those nurseries. Amos senior's obituary in the *Gardeners' Chronicle* of 14 June 1913 (at the grand age of 72) made mention of his 'two sons and three daughters, both sons are engaged in the [nursery] business which will be carried on under its present name'. One of those sons was, of course, the Amos Perry that would eventually make his name in chrysanthemums, as well as irises.

'Our' Amos Perry had no doubts as to his career and was a nurseryman from the outset. He travelled widely in Britain and on the Continent to look for new plants and by 1930 he had already gained about a hundred awards from the Royal Horticultural Society for plants which he had introduced or bred; thus he was excellently placed to spot the possibilities of the *Chrysanthemum* x *rubellum*. Anxious to spread the Perry family around, Amos Perry gave family names to many of the plants he bred, including the irises 'Peggy Perry', 'Marcus Perry', 'Mrs Perry' and 'Roger Perry'; and so it seems ironic that his most famous chrysanthemum should be 'Clara Curtis', a naming whose origins are now lost. There was a plant hunter of the name of Charles Curtis (1853–1928) who worked for the Veitch & Sons nursery where Amos Perry's great-grandfather had worked, and one can only presume that a long-term family friendship had arisen. Charles Curtis, who joined the Veitch nursery in 1874, was sent to search for new plants in Madagascar, Borneo and Java, and eventually settled in Penang, where he became head of the botanic gardens there. Ill health eventually forced retirement in Devon, where instead of orchids and pitcher plants he devoted himself to less exotic carnations and sweet peas until his death in 1923, but whether he had a wife or daughter (or granddaughter) by the name of Clara is not known.

Amos Perry's *Chrysanthemum* x *rubellum* 'Clara Curtis'.

A similar mystery surrounds the naming of the hybrid Rubellum chrysanthemum 'Mary Stoker', a profuse flowering cultivar with a soft apricot colour. Now technically named *Chrysanthemum zawadskii* var. *latilobum* 'Mary Stoker' (and for a short while *Dendranthema* 'Mary Stoker'), 'Mary Stoker' vies with 'Clara Curtis' and the shell-pink 'Anna Hay' for the most popular of the hardy garden chrysanthemums alongside the rather more easily explained chrysanthemum 'Autumn Bronze'. In the 1930s *The Times Survey of Gardening* wrote of the Perry Rubellums that they

> outshine even the various Korean strains in hardiness, range of colour and freedom of growth. They seem to flower unchecked no matter how hard the autumn nip, and to grow them in a roadside garden is to invite an almost embarrassing degree of attention and enquiry from passers-by.[1]

Other nurserymen names forever associated with the chrysanthemum in England have been explored by the plant writer Judith

Taylor and more recently still by Judy Barker. They include Henry Cannell (1833–1914) of Swanley, Kent, who sent specimens of his chrysanthemums to the plant trials at Cornell University, New York, in 1897, along with fellow nurseryman William Bull. Also William Clibran & Son, who traded from the late nineteenth century until the 1960s, with seed warehouses and nurseries across the Lancashire and Cheshire areas. William Robinson (of Gravetye Manor) reported on Clibran's success with their 'cut singles' of chrysanthemum flowers in *The Garden* periodical of 1900 and again in 1902 when their winning entry with silver gilt medal was 'Nemeskat'. Another winner in both of those years was a Mr Robert Foster of Nunhead Cemetery, presumably the cemetery keeper making money on the side from selling suitable funerary flowers in 'spare space' until needed for burial. This was a frequent hobby or side-line of cemetery attendants, and was encouraged as it gave a cemetery a gay and attractive air. Also recorded by William Robinson in the 1890s was W. J. Godfrey, who ran the Exmouth Nurseries in Devon that showed the cultivars 'Miss Dorothy Shea', 'Charles Blick' (named after another nurseryman), 'Duchess of Devonshire', and, rather more poetically, 'Aureole Virginale'. Godfrey also showed 'Monsieur Chas Molin', introduced from France in 1894, and inevitably his own 'Mrs W. J. Godfrey'. Many of his chrysanthemums were also named from his nursery location of Exmouth, including 'Exmouth Crimson' and 'Exmouth Rival'.

Dedication was the byword of these early nurserymen and chrysanthemum growers, and none more than Robert Owen (1840–1897), whose prize cultivars included 'Magicienne', 'Princess of Wales' and the incurved 'Lord Rosebery'. Owen passed away aged only 57 while working in the chrysanthemum glasshouses at his nursery. His assistant commented that by the time he had realized anything was wrong Owen was already dead, survived by his chrysanthemum namesake 'Owen's Perfection'. Larger nurseries also added chrysanthemums to their general output, including the Veitch nurseries in Exeter and London which, according to James Morton (an American author of an 1881 book on chrysanthemums), 'imported from Japan six new sorts, called "Ben d'Or", "Comte de Germiny [*sic*]", "Duchess of Connaught", "Thunberg", and others, all of which are well known'. In Europe, nurserymen included Karl Foerster, another son of a nurseryman, who published an article on Japanese chrysanthemums for dry gardens in 1909 and developed the cultivars 'Brennpunkt', 'Citronella' and 'Goldmarianne' (the last named after his daughter). Unfortunately his work was cut short by the advent of the First World War in 1914.[2]

Although the chrysanthemum was beloved of many a relatively humble glasshouse owner or member of a chrysanthemum society, it also had its wealthy devotees. In 1883 at the palatial house and garden of the Duke of Newcastle at Worksop Manor there were said to be more than 250 chrysanthemum plants comprised of 115 varieties, varying in height from 0.5 to 2.5 metres (18 in. to 8 ft) with blooms so fine and perfect and large enough to be the size of show dahlias. Both the budding technique (where all but six buds were removed) and the 'natural' growing style were practised by the gardener at Worksop Manor, a Mr Sutton, and the results were reported in the *Gardeners' Chronicle* on 17 November 1883.[3]

The gardens of Leopold de Rothschild at Ascott in Buckinghamshire were also famed for their year-round displays, including autumn and winter periods. In 1913 a writer for the *Gardeners' Chronicle* visited during the winter period to admire the plants that had been persuaded to flower at that usually blank time in the gardener's calendar. In a typical mix of respectful praise for the upper classes and flowery breathless description of their horticultural successes, the writer noted that

> Mr Leopold de Rothschild holds that the first essential in successful gardening is for the owner to decide what he wants and the time and season at which he requires the chief display . . . This plan is adopted in all the famous gardens of this enthusiastic amateur horticulturist, and although flowers are plentiful at all seasons of the year the main show in

In the early 20th century the Rothschild family collected new chrysanthemum varieties in their gardens, and old chrysanthemum china similar to this in their display cabinets.

each garden is timed for the season at which it is most required. Ascott Gardens, Leighton Buzzard, for many years under the management of Mr John Jennings, has become famous for its display of winter flowers.[4]

Among that display of surprising salvias and out-of-season lemons were, of course, the chrysanthemums which Leopold Rothschild (and his gardener) had held back by pinching and cooling until the desired effect was gained at the season chosen. Inside the house, Leopold's son Anthony also introduced a collection of oriental ceramics. This collection mostly consisted of Ming (1386–1644) and K'ang Hsi (1662–1722) wares. It also was especially marked for the so-called 'san ts'ai' (three colour) wares of the late Ming Dynasty.[5] Elegant bowls and vases with flowing chrysanthemums in vibrant shades of blue, purple and burnt yellow echoed the displays that his father had created in the glasshouses.

Rothschild chrysanthemums also inspired the businessman Ambrose Congreve (1907–2011), who went on to create the garden at Mount Congreve (near Kilmeaden, Co. Waterford), where chrysanthemums were grown in rows in the walled garden and picked for the house, cared for by some of the seventy gardeners employed on the Congreve estate. On his one-hundredth birthday Ambrose Congreve quoted the old proverb: 'To be happy for an hour, have a glass of wine. To be happy for a day, read a book. To be happy for a week, take a wife. To be happy forever, make a garden', to which he could have appended the Chinese version: 'If you would be happy for a lifetime, grow chrysanthemums.'

At home in the luxurious surroundings of Ascott or Worksop, the hardy chrysanthemum – along with roses, currant bushes, peas, cauliflowers, carrots and cabbages – was also grown in the gardens of the politically contrasting Clousden Hill Free Communist and Co-operative Colony just outside Newcastle upon Tyne. The Clousden Hill colonists were encouraged in their work by the utopian ideals of William Morris (better known generally for his Arts and Crafts designs) and the Russian anarchist, Peter Kropotkin. Work on the colony was hard and long but despite the relief of adding beauty to utility (as Morris would have said) the colony collapsed in just three years, only lasting from 1895 to 1898.[6]

Away from the gritty realities of co-operative toil, the chrysanthemum was a popular flower throughout the Edwardian period and into the post-war period with the first of the London chrysanthemum shows held at the Royal Horticultural Society Halls, Westminster, in 1921, by which time there was a chrysanthemum society in nearly every town. But the return of wartime conditions in 1939 concentrated minds on other aspects of the garden and greenhouses were left unheated or commandeered for tomatoes and salad crops.

Britain joined the then European war at the start of September in
1939. The Royal Horticultural Society Great Autumn Show, due to
be held just ten days later, was immediately cancelled and all over
the country flowerbeds full of chrysanthemums were dug up to
make way for autumn sowings of vegetables, as recorded by Stephen
Cheveley, the gardening correspondent for *The Times*, in his book
A Garden Goes to War.

In 1939 Cheveley had relatively recently moved into a suburban
London house with a large garden, a relief from his previous struggles
with a windswept garden on the coast of North Yorkshire. His move
had allowed him to plant a plot measuring two-thirds of an acre with
hardy plants of all kinds, as well as a small, discrete 'out of the way
piece' for some herbs, a few onions and marrows. However, the newly
launched Dig for Victory campaign (initially known as the Grow
More campaign) relied on gardening writers such as Cheveley setting
an example to the general populace, and so the flowers had to go. In
a patriotic fervour Cheveley describes the fateful day with as much
cheerfulness as he could muster:

> On a Saturday afternoon, early in September, my young son
> and I cleared the border. We cut off all flowers worth taking
> into the house; whole plants of chrysanthemums were exe-
> cuted, and they made a glorious bunch in a huge bowl in the
> hall. After the first unhappy twinges of regret we became
> keen on the job, and once the flowers were out of the way it
> didn't seem nearly so bad.

It would appear that Cheveley was among those who collected
the new chrysanthemum types, perhaps those that had come from
the nursery of Amos Perry, as he continues:

> The new chrysanthemums were lifted, and replanted close
> together in two rows at one end of the border. Here they will,
> at any rate, survive until happier times return, and they can

be restored to a more worthy position. The other plants were lifted bodily, their roots freed from soil by banging with the back of the spade, and taken to the compost heap.[7]

The 'happier times' Cheveley envisioned were to be in 'a year or two', when everything would be 'restor[ed] to its former beauty' and plants could be increased by dividing the clumps that had been happy in their temporary spots.[8] In fact it would be five long years before the chrysanthemums were allowed back into their flower borders, by which time they may well have outgrown the small areas allocated for these memories of happier times.

For the nurseryman Amos Perry, the timing of his new hybrid Rubellum chrysanthemum 'Clara Curtis' was unfortunate, coinciding with the outbreak of Second World War food-production campaigns. Flower nurseries were instructed to reduce their stocks to a mere 30 per cent of pre-war stocks, and as the war dragged on, as low as 10 per cent, with the rest turned over to peas and cabbages; only the most dedicated or fortunate came through the war with the majority of their cultivars surviving.

With their strong association with working-men's flower societies, chrysanthemums and dahlias fared especially badly during the war as regulations forbad the planting or growing of any flowers on wartime allotments. So dire was the situation that the Bolton and District Horticultural and Chrysanthemum Society joined forces with the Bolton Allotments Society and the County Borough of Bolton to put on a wartime exhibition of vegetables in September 1941, with not a hint of a chrysanthemum. However, as soon as restrictions were loosened in 1944 many societies were quick to re-form. In a spirit of optimism, the Cambridge and District Chrysanthemum Society was founded in 1947, and in 1949 the National Chrysanthemum Society noted that more than 2,000 new members had enrolled across the country. As soon after the war as 1946 a Mr Goddard brought out a manual on growing *Early Flowering Chrysanthemums*, while in 1949 F. W. Allerton published *Chrysanthemums for Amateur and Market*

Liege _Chromolith L Severeyns Michel

This 19th-century Belgian illustration of 'Chrysanthemum sinense, var. japanense' contains the 'Japanese' naming that would be quietly dropped in the 1940s and '50s.

Grower, suggesting they were still popular for flower arrangements and weddings. This latter use may be a clue to their continued popularity, as weddings were as popular during wartime and immediately post-war as flowers were rare.

Restrictions on flower growing, and indeed wholesale destruction of flower-plant stocks as part of the Dig for Victory campaign, had led to severe shortages of some flowers, especially roses and bulb flowers, and chrysanthemums stepped into the breach. Quick to grow back and also relatively easily available from amateur stocks, they were the obvious flower of the moment; add in their longevity and ability to flower through several months of the year and the result was many a 1950s 'chrysanthemum wedding' regardless of where their original homeland had been. It seems slightly odd that a flower whose homeland was Japan should have flourished in England in the immediate aftermath of the war, a period when many of the Japanese-style gardens created in the Edwardian and inter-war period were targeted for destruction. However, as sites such as Gatton Park in Surrey had their tea temples burnt and Japanese stone lanterns toppled into lily ponds, the chrysanthemum still survived in flower shows across the land. Although it is notable that the term 'Japanese Chrysanthemum' so often used in the Victorian and Edwardian eras appears to have been quietly dropped in many chrysanthemum publications of the period.

Not usually known for their reticence in claiming superiority, American nurseries and flower fanciers of the 1850s and '60s had to acknowledge that in regard to chrysanthemums the nurseries of France, Belgium and England had stolen a march on them. There is no authentic record and not even a 'founding myth' of who first introduced the chrysanthemum to America, although as it was in Europe by the later eighteenth century, and firmly established in English flower borders by the 1830s, then surely a late eighteenth or very early nineteenth century date must be guessed at.

The first mention of chrysanthemums being exhibited in America is in the rather unglamorous periodical the *New England Farmer* of

26 November 1830. This gave a report of chrysanthemums being shown at the Massachusetts Horticultural Society on 20 November of that year, including some well-known 'English' varieties including 'Tasseled White', 'Park's Small Yellow', 'Quilled Lilac', 'Quilled White' and 'Golden Lotus'. The cultivar namings indicate that the origin of the chrysanthemum infiltration was most likely England and not direct from China or Japan or via the continent.[9] An American catalogue of 1857 refers to the 'magnificent seminal varieties' latterly produced in Europe (thanks to the special trading relationship with Japan and China) and goes on to indicate that chrysanthemums were now filling the gardens of the middle and southern states, where they supplied 'one of the principal adornments by an ever-varying display of beauty during the autumnal period when most other plants present us only [with] the remains of departed verdure'. They were also grown in the greenhouses of those states where they prefaced the later-flowering plants. Names of varieties available by 1857 indicate an influx of European varieties by this period alongside the original English colonists; these varieties included 'Duchess d'Abrantes', 'Grand Napoleon', 'Guillaume Tell', 'General Lafont de Villiers' and 'La Superba', alongside the English 'Annie Salter', 'Annie Henderson' and the 'Cloth of Gold' (a suitably fine yellow colour).

By the mid-1860s Japanese varieties had also come direct to America courtesy of the nurseryman Peter Henderson (1822–1890). Henderson was said to have a *Grandiflorum* 'very large with peculiar strap shaped petals, golden yellow and very double', a *Laciniatum*, beautifully fringed and 'a great favourite with the ladies', and a *Japonicum*, 'with remarkable twilled petals in orange and brown, standing erect whilst the whole flower nods, making it look precisely like a rich tassel'. Why this latter was not also a favourite with the ladies, like the fringed *Laciniatum*, is not explained.[10]

Henderson was born in Scotland in 1822, emigrated to America to try his luck in 1843, and set up as a market gardener in Jersey City. Despite the interruption of the Civil War (1861–5), forcing him to move to South Bergen, he published his first book, entitled *Gardening*

Peter Henderson & Co. carried on specializing in chrysanthemums after the death of its founder in 1890, as evidenced by this 1902 advertisement.

for Profit, in 1865 and followed it up with *Practical Floriculture* in 1868, which ran to numerous editions. Specializing in seeds and plants especially suited to the American climates (now referred to as Zones), Henderson became one of the most important seed traders. He introduced the American public to the world of lithographed colour catalogues and become one of the first to employ the motif of an older white-haired gentleman to establish the credentials of the merchandise – a motif used many times since. He became known as the father of American horticulture and ornamental gardening, and during the course of his 45-year career, much of it trading as Peter Henderson & Company, he is said to have written more than 175,000 letters to his customers, bringing a personal touch to the business.

In his book *Practical Floriculture* Henderson gave a detailed record of how he grew the various types of chrysanthemum, including a diary of daily operations of planting and budding. Under the heading 'Construction of Bouquets' Henderson also gives an insight into the popularity of the chrysanthemum in America, stating

> At present in the fall and early winter months the Chrysanthemums are perhaps used to a greater extent than any other flower. In the months of November and December nearly every other well-dressed lady to be met with on the fashionable streets of New York, is found wearing a corsage bouquet

In the 20th century the U.S. embraced the chrysanthemum with spectacular shows and conservatory winter gardens, as shown here in a display from Bronx Park, New York.

of chrysanthemums, and from their great range of colour, almost every shade of dress can be matched except blue.[11]

That elusive blue chrysanthemum again!

Raising chrysanthemums from seed, and thus freeing oneself from the nurseries and tradesman, is always one of the aims of the flower fancier; and just as the first chrysanthemum raised from seed in England was celebrated, so too with America. It was Dr H. P. Walcott, of Cambridge, Massachusetts, who was able to exhibit seedlings raised from his own garden plants at the Autumn 1879 Massachusetts Horticultural Society in Boston and move forward the hybridization of chrysanthemums in the USA. By the 1880s American nurseries had joined with Europe in breeding new cultivars, including the 'charming novelties' which were to give rise to the multiple show classes that mark out the chrysanthemum. F. R. Pierson of Tarrytown, New York, introduced what was to become one of the most popular of the Japanese chrysanthemums, named the 'Queen of Autumn', and in the same decade John Thorpe (1842–1891) took up the work started by Dr Walcott.

Known as the 'father of the chrysanthemum' in America, the avuncular John Thorpe had been influenced as a child by Samuel Broome, head gardener at the Inner Temple who made the gardens famous for their chrysanthemums. Born in Keyham, Leicestershire, into a family of gardeners and nurserymen, Thorpe had trained in Glasgow and Stratford upon Avon before moving to Cleveland, Ohio, and then New York, where he worked for the firm of W. Hallock & Sons. His skills in horticulture and his experience of British flower societies led him to become first the secretary of the New York Horticultural Society and then the president of the American Society of Florists who, according to a *Chicago Tribune* issue of 1891, presented him with a gold watch and chain for his pains.

Although skilled with all sorts of plants (he was said to have carried off first honours in all 48 classes in the 1885 New York Show), Thorpe specialized in pinks and chrysanthemums. In November 1884 he published an article entitled simply 'Chrysanthemums' in the fashionable and influential *Harper's Magazine*, resulting in an increase in the flower's popularity, and in 1890 he founded the Chrysanthemum Society of America, which resulted in an explosion of different cultivars and varieties. By 1905 there were more than 3,000 varieties of chrysanthemum listed by the Chrysanthemum Society of America, a society which the writer Arthur Herrington claimed (in language perhaps more appropriate for a Nobel Peace Prize than a chrysanthemum society) as working for 'the common good of all interested, and making history that future generations will justly appreciate';[12] but then the chrysanthemum does encourage one to hyperbole.

Thorpe obviously cared more for the outward show of his chrysanthemums than his own appearance and was described by the *Chicago Tribune* in 1891 as 'as simple and unassuming as an old farmer', caring nothing for dress.[13] Just to confuse matters there seems to have been an earlier American nurseryman named John Thorpe (active in the 1820s) who specialized in fruit trees and appears in what is known as the 'The Paragon Apple Muddle'. This episode in the pomological history of America was caused by the apple Paragon, also known as the Blacktwig or Mammoth Blacktwig or Winesap, being somehow re-bred in a different state — resulting in what was meant to be a separate variety of Arkansas Big Blacktwig in the 1880s. However, to be honest the plot of the whole episode, including several nurserymen and at least four different cultivars of Blacktwig all also known as Winesaps (but only some of which were Paragons), is perhaps best left for a future crime writer looking for a complex, twisted tale and although compelling is only relevant to the chrysanthemum story as a warning to avoid a confusion of John Thorpes.

Back with American chrysanthemum fanciers and the correct John Thorpe, the stage was set for the commercial growing of the chrysanthemum in the USA. This was eventually to be achieved by the Enomoto brothers from Japan, who set themselves up in California in the 1880s. The Californian climate was ideal for the Japanese chrysanthemum and by 1910, coinciding with the height of the craze

BARBARA BROMFIELD

YELLOW
LILLIAN
DOTY

CRIMSON
GLORY

Hardy Chrysanthemums *(See page 87)*
10610 One each of these seven good, strong plants for $2.00. **Postpaid.**

An American spring catalogue, dated 1927, looks forward to the riches of the autumn.

for all things Japanese on both sides of the Atlantic, the Enomoto were sending flowers across the USA, overshadowing the efforts of amateurs who in many regions of America were hampered by the lack of hardiness. In the 1930s the crossing of C. *indicum* with C. *zawadskii coreanum* and C. *japonicum* by the Connecticut breeder Alex Cummings (originally from Scotland) gave rise to the hardier 'Korean' chrysanthemum in a similar manner to the work of Perry Amos in England on the x *rubellums* (the hybridized strain).

One of the plants used in Cummings's breeding programme had been collected by the plant hunter Ernest 'Chinese' Wilson (1876–1930) while on an expedition to northern Korea for the Arnold Arboretum. In general, the Korean hybrids are shorter and bushier than the x *rubellums*, with the popular 'Ruby Mound', with its deep-red double flowers, only growing to about 45 centimetres (18 in.) tall and even the slightly taller 'Wedding Day' only 55 centimetres (21½ in.). The latter appears to have been named by someone with a romantic touch as the white petals surround a vibrant yellow-green centre which fades to cream as the flowers age. Original 1930s cultivars included 'Apollo' in the red/bronze of the setting sun, 'Mercury' in salmon and 'Mars' in wine-red, although one wonders if Bacchus might have been more appropriate for this?

By the time these dwarf chrysanthemums appeared, the role of the commercial flower industry was well established, and with the arrival of the 1930 Plant Patent Act in America these new plants could be 'protected' by patent. Until the entry of Japan into the Second World War and the bombing of Pearl Harbor, the chrysanthemum was to reign supreme as the 'Fall flower' in America as it did in England, with the wonderfully named 'Mums from Minnesota' being commercially bred by Dick Lehman and Dr Ezra Jacob Kraus (a retired professor of botany). Even after the entry of Japan into the war the flower was not as reviled as might have been expected given that many of the specialist breeders had links with both East and West, among them the men that would become internees at Gila River War Relocation Center.

From May 1942 until its closure on 16 November 1945 (two months after the dropping of the atomic bombs on Nagasaki and Hiroshima), the Gila River Relocation Center in Arizona acted as an incarceration centre for Japanese Americans from the West Coast and Hawaii. Constructed within the Gila River Indian reservation, despite strong objections by the reservation's Gila River Indian Community, the camp held more than 13,000 people (although designed for only 10,000) and became the fourth-largest settlement site in Arizona. With only a single watchtower and no barbed wire it was perhaps the least oppressive of the internment camps, although conditions were harsh and there were many deaths both in the camp and among people travelling to it across the Arizona desert lands. The people that came together in the camps were from a wide range of backgrounds, including photographers, artists, actors, (American) soldiers, scientists and even baseball players.

Activities within the camps reflected its varied inhabitants' interests, with facilities provided by the state and the incarcerated

A Japanese internee tending chrysanthemums in the unpromising soil of the Arizona desert in the Gila River War Relocation Center.

The craze for chrysanthemums was used to raise funds for war widows and children in Belgium in 1914.

themselves. Recreations included sport, theatre, art, lectures in a wide range of subjects including 'social graces', and also chrysanthemum growing. Despite needing precious water, and protection from the extremes of both heat and cold, chrysanthemums were grown in the sandy soils in the traditional mat layout of Japanese chrysanthemum

Longwood Gardens, Pennsylvania, is famed for its annual chrysanthemum festival, housed in the splendours of the 1920s conservatory.

houses. Wooden slatted shade houses were constructed and watering was done by hand with watering cans. When he visited the Gila River Relocation Center in November 1942 the war photographer Francis Stewart recorded many rare and patented flowers being developed by the 'firm' of Nakata & Son in the centre's 'hothouses'. Itaro Nakata was a former worker at an experimental nursery in Tracy, California, with more than twenty years of experience in the nursery business, and he spent his time in Gila River developing (and later patenting) new types of chrysanthemum. Sadly Stewart captured Itaro not with chrysanthemums but with choice specimens of larkspurs grown at the nursery. Other internees grew vegetables and fruits, or helped with the cows, and there were seed specialists and farmers in the camp alongside the scientists and sportsmen, including S. Hanasaki, a former vegetable seed specialist from San Jose, California, where he owned his own business and sold under the trade name of 'Lucky Seeds', which seems to have been an inappropriate name in the circumstances.

In the late twentieth and early twenty-first centuries, chrysanthemums made a return to the American flower festival scene, including Yoder Brothers Inc. – nurserymen and breeders who specialized in autumn-hardy chrysanthemums for the all-important 'fall' market. Perhaps more famously among the general public the chrysanthemum appears at the Longwood Gardens in Pennsylvania, with its 1.6-hectare (4-ac) grand conservatory or winter garden. Chrysanthemums were first grown and displayed in the Longwood Gardens when founder Pierre S. du Pont opened the conservatory in 1921, and today it hosts thousands of colourful chrysanthemum blooms, including the one-of-a-kind Thousand Bloom Chrysanthemum (in 2017 actually boasting 1,443 blooms and measuring 3.7 metres wide by 2.4 metres tall (12 by 8 ft)). Visitors through October and November are rewarded not only with the magnificent flowerheads but Chinese lanterns and Chinese music in the conservatory.[14] The annual Chrysanthemum Festival showcases the traditional Asian art of cultivating chrysanthemums into grand artistic shapes and more than seventy large-scale topiary forms – some trained for more than a year to resemble clouds, balls, spirals and pagodas – and columns of cascading blooms welcome visitors. A similarly stunning chrysanthemum garden appears to have been maintained at Hanford in California in the early twentieth century, although the black-and-white postcards give only a pale reflection of its glories.

The 'Pont Japonais' at Giverny reflects Monet's fascination with the East.

five

An Impression of Chrysanthemums

❦

I n 1890 the dramatist and art critic Octave Mirbeau (1848–1917) wrote to his friend and fellow plant lover Claude Monet:

> If you can send me a few more dahlias, yes, I would like that, And next year I'll make you a collection of chrysanthemums I have which are all wonderful with crazy shapes and beautiful colours, I found them at a brilliant gardeners in Le Vaudreuil.[1]

Their correspondence reflected the fascination that the Impressionist artist-gardeners had for the exotic chrysanthemum. Monet collected Japanese prints and ceramics, which also appear in his paintings at Giverny and still decorate the house there. His collection included more than two hundred prints by the famous Japanese artists Hokusai (1760–1849), Hiroshige (1797–1858) and Utamaro (1753–1806), including their portrayal of the revered chrysanthemum. Chrysanthemums were an especial favourite of Monet (1840–1926) with their links to Japan and Japanese art traditions. Photographs record the visit to the Giverny gardens by Monsieur Kuroki and his wife, relatives of the leading Japanese collector of Impressionist paintings, Kojiro Matsukata, and it was the Japanese tradition of water gardens and bridges that inspired Monet's own pond with its famous water lilies, which was named in an early photograph titled 'Pont Japonais'.

Other Oriental plants favoured by Monet included bamboo, tree peony and the delicate blooms of the Japanese cherry trees. Monet used his gardens to experiment with colours and hues as well as horticulture, indeed the writer Marcel Proust famously recorded that Giverny was a 'garden of tones and colours even more than of flowers, a garden which must be less the former florist-garden than, if I can put it that way, a colourist-garden'.[2] Chrysanthemums were the perfect autumn flower for this effect, especially when planted in the bold masses that Monet favoured. He relished the texture and harmonious colours of the large heads and, as well as producing still-lifes of the flowers in vases and jugs, he created several canvases full of almost abstract jostling blooms that seem to float on the canvas in the same way that the water lilies float on the water and the sky. Between 1878 and 1883, working from Argenteuil, then Veteuil and eventually at Giverny, Claude Monet produced some twenty floral still-lifes – including four entirely focused on the chrysanthemum.

Among the bouquet of chrysanthemum-loving French Impressionists was the artist and gardener Gustave Caillebotte (1848–1894), based at Petit-Gennevilliers. Coming from a wealthy family, Caillebotte never had the fear of financial collapse and deprivation that had haunted Monet, but he shared with him a love of all things horticultural. Petit-Gennevilliers was a suburb of Paris on the banks of the Seine, close to Monet's old village of Argenteuil, and the gardens there benefitted from the soil, the moisture and the particular light conditions that also inspired Monet. Caillebotte had acquired the house in 1881 and moved there permanently in 1888, aged forty. From an upper-class family background in Paris, he had started painting and drawing when the family bought a second country property in Yerres, also to the south of Paris. A law degree was followed by the army draft in the Franco-Prussian war, before he returned to a life in art.

By 1874 Caillebotte was exhibiting his work and in 1876 his famous painting *The Floor Scrapers* was shown in the second large Impressionist exhibition, along with seven of his other paintings.

Claude Monet, *Massif de chrysanthèmes* (Bed of Chrysanthemum), 1897, oil on canvas.

His style was realist but with a softness that often bears comparison with painters such as Pissarro or Renoir, with pastel overtones. Freed from the need to sell his works by inheriting a share of his mother's family fortune early on in his career in 1878, he stopped exhibiting at the age of 34. However, his output remained constant if not prolific until around 1890 and featured subjects such as urban scenes, picnics, boating and still-lifes including florals. After the move to Petit-Gennevilliers, he increasingly devoted himself to gardening as well as building and racing yachts and entertaining friends, including Renoir, while helping to fund fellow artists and even paying at one time for a studio for Monet (as well as purchasing his pictures).

Caillebotte was in some ways a more serious gardener than many of his artist companions. His gardens included walled productive areas as famously depicted in his paintings, and areas devoted to the cultivation of specific plants rather than the aesthetics of the flowerbed. The hothouses of Petit-Gennevilliers were home to Caillebotte's increasing collection of orchids, and when he could finally afford his own

Gustave Caillebotte, *Chrysanthemums in the Garden at Petit-Gennevilliers*, 1893, oil on canvas.

glasshouses, Monet asked Caillebotte's advice on the construction of a new one at Giverny, enquiring as to whether Caillebotte felt glass or wood was the best, a discussion which gardeners still have today. The rest of the gardens overflowed with roses and irises as well as areas set aside for dahlias and of course the new arrivals of Japanese chrysanthemums.

Caillebotte's most famous image of chrysanthemums, painted in 1893 (now in the Metropolitan Museum of Art in New York), was titled *Chrysanthemums in the Garden at Petit-Gennevilliers*, making it clear that these are plants grown in the gardens and not bought in as a still-life 'prop'. It is an unusual close-up view of densely packed blossoms in colours ranging from white through yellows, golds and apricots to plums and rubies. The heads hang heavy and the grey-green foliage appears slightly wilted, as if battered by the sun of Normandy. As with so many of Caillebotte's paintings, the viewer is at an odd angle to the subject, raised and slightly slanting, and the mass is cut off on the top right and the left as if to admit defeat when trying to crowd them all in. It is possible that Caillebotte was playing with the odd perspective needed for some decorative door panels, which are often viewed from above or below. He may well have been echoing the fruit and flower panels that Monet painted for the Impressionist's art dealer Durand-Ruel and which Caillebotte 'copied' with orchid panels on his own doors (although some of Caillebotte's urban paintings, for example, are also from a slanted perspective looking down).

A rather different painting of chrysanthemums, less full and with tones of whitish blues and browns, was accomplished by Caillebotte in the same year, entitled *White and Yellow Chrysanthemums, 1893* (Musée Marmottan, Paris).[3] This painting belonged to Monet during his lifetime. In return Caillebotte owned a still-life of chrysanthemums by Monet, one of those rejected by France in the bequest settlement following Monet's death in 1926. Caillebotte also painted cut chrysanthemums, as Monet had done earlier in his career, most famously in a group of several Japanese ceramics on a bamboo woven table.

A focus on close-up masses of chrysanthemum heads in a range of tones and hues, as seen in Caillebotte's paintings, also appears, albeit with the addition of a woman, in a canvas by Jacques-Joseph Tissot, commonly known as James Tissot (1836–1902), an artist on the fringe of the Impressionists. Tissot had been a society portrait painter in Paris before moving to London in 1871, where he mixed portraiture with constant – almost obsessive – painting of his mistress Kathleen Newton (1854–1882) and their garden in St John's Wood. In 1874 Edmond de Goncourt wrote of Tissot that he had 'a studio with a waiting room where, at all times, there is iced champagne at the disposal of visitors'.[4] The house was large and the gardens both extensive and elaborate with an iron colonnade, modelled on the Parc Monceau, around a large pool. A covered glass walkway gave entrance into the garden, which was later to be featured in *Country Life* during the residence of the painter Lawrence Alma-Tadema. Tissot was not a practical gardener himself, employing instead a man who was described as gardening 'in a footman's livery and silk stockings' to keep the gardens in a fashionable style.

The chrysanthemums featured in Tissot's 1874/5 painting of that name are brighter and clearer than those of Caillebotte: whites, lemon yellows and light oranges stand proud with smaller heads and only the occasional one bowed down with its own weight. They are planted in pots rather than the earth (as Caillebotte's later plants also appear to be) and were most probably standing in one of the winter gardens or conservatories of Tissot's house, safely protected with glass from any buffeting winds or strong heat.

The woman in this painting, sometimes referred to as being 'in gardening clothes', has been suggested as being Kathleen Newton, Tissot's Irish muse and model, who was to die from consumption at the tragically early age of 28. Before she met Tissot, Kate had already been sent out from England to be married in India, divorced (on the grounds of non-consumption), and had then become pregnant by a man she despised and refused to marry, giving birth to a daughter as a single woman back in London. The slightly ginger hair and pale

James Tissot, *Chrysanthemums, c.* 1875, oil on canvas.

skin perhaps suggest Irish origins and also complement the hues of the flowers, as does her pale yellow bonnet and shawl, with a black scarf denoting the cold of the late autumn day. However, the 1874/5 date given for the painting does not tie in with the use of Kathleen as the model. Although she probably became Tissot's mistress around the time of this painting, giving birth to their son Cecil in 1876, she only modelled for him after the birth of Cecil. The novelist Lucy Paquette, writer of a fictionalized life of Tissot, has identified the model for this 1874/5 painting as being the same woman who appears in several paintings of around 1874, but she remains sadly unnamed.

After a life almost as eventful as Kathleen's own, travelling between owners in London, South Africa, London again, and America, the painting is now in the Clark Art Institute in Williamstown, Massachusetts. Chrysanthemums also appear in a later work by Tissot called *A Widow*, where their white flowers are symbols of death and contrast with the black dress of the bereaved young wife.

Before we leave the gardener-painters of France we should note the connections between French art and one of the most famous English gardens, at Munstead Wood, Surrey. Munstead Wood was the home of the garden designer Gertrude Jekyll (1843–1932), whose articles in *Country Life* were well known to Claude Monet and whose books were on the shelves at Giverny. Jekyll had started out as an artist and craftswoman rather than a horticulturalist, but had gradually shifted focus – rather literally as her eyesight became increasingly poor and her working relationship with the architect Edwin Lutyens increasingly successful.

Both in her own garden and in those of her clients, Jekyll suggested plants that could provide drifts of hues and tones in the style seen in the canvases of Impressionist chrysanthemums. Jekyll did not have extensive glasshousing and her planting therefore relied on more hardy plants, so that rather than the Japanese chrysanthemum her favourites for autumn included Michaelmas daisies (of which she bred her own varieties) and the *Chrysanthemum maximum* or Shasta daisy (now *Leucanthemum maximum*), with its brilliant white heads and yellow eyes. Still among one of the most popular of the 'cottage garden' plants, the Shasta daisy grows to almost 1 metre (3 ft) tall, with a sturdy appearance and deep green foliage, making it ideal for the mixed flower border. Unlike the meadow ox-eye daisy, it is not invasive and will not swamp other plants or droop when overcrowded, holding its clear blooms up sturdily. It can even be 'dressed up or down' for more or less sophisticated effects as noted by the Royal Horticultural Society and the BBC Gardening Guide, who say of Shastas, 'Team them with herbaceous perennials such as *Lychnis coronaria*, scabious or pinks for a cottage garden combination, or use them with silver or grey foliage such as artemisia and gypsophila for a more sophisticated association.'[5] The RHS-recommended cultivar 'Snowcap' produces a clear bright white bloom, bringing a freshness ideal for a June to September flowering.

From England to America we add another Impressionist artist, again under the influence of the long reach of Monet. Dennis Miller Bunker (1861–1890) was an American artist of oils and watercolours who had studied at the Ecole nationale supérieure des Beaux-Arts in Paris. From here he had travelled each summer to the French countryside and through Normandy. In 1888 he spent the summer in England working with John Singer Sargent (1856–1925), whom he had met the previous year when Sargent toured America. His influences were Impressionist and his subjects landscapes and portraits, with many of the latter painted outside. Bunker had struggled at first to put the influences of Sargent into practice, and complained to his friend and patron Mrs Isabella Gardner that he had 'ruins of numerous works, for I've not been idle', but none that satisfied.[6]

No paintings survive from the summer spent with Sargent but once back in Boston the influence of that summer became evident and Bunker produced many of his best works, including *In the Greenhouse* (*c.* 1888), *The Pool, Medfield* (1889) and, of course, *Chrysanthemums* (1888). The chrysanthemums in question flourished in the gardens and glasshouses of the same Isabella Gardner (1840–1924). Mrs Gardner loved flowers and gardening (and art), and the Bunker family's summer residence at Green Hill, Brookline (in Boston, Massachusetts) boasted extravagant displays. Bunker gave this work to Gardner, calling it 'A very poor sketch of your favourite flower – and which was painted entirely to please you.' Despite the painting's importance as one of the earliest examples of American Impressionism, Mrs Gardner was not much interested in Impressionist landscapes. In the early 1890s John Singer Sargent alerted her to the upcoming sale of a famous Monet painting, but she never pursued it, although she acquired portraits by Degas and Manet and in 1906 visited Claude Monet at Giverny, an event she found 'perfect in every way'.[7]

Tragically, Bunker died aged only 29, and he and his works were long neglected. In 2016 the Royal Academy of Arts (London) exhibition 'Painting the Modern Garden: Monet to Matisse' included Bunker's *Chrysanthemums* – indicative of a much-deserved revival of interest in this innovative American Impressionist artist and, incidentally, the chrysanthemum. The picture is now in the collection of the Isabella Stewart Gardner Museum in Boston alongside paintings

Dennis Miller Bunker, *Chrysanthemums*, 1888, oil on canvas.

Mathias J. Alten. *Chrysanthemums*, 1896, oil on canvas. The painting is unusual in its spidery arrangement.

by Sargent and several portraits of Isabella Gardner herself. The extraordinary courtyard of the Museum reflects Mrs Gardner's passion for gardens and seasonal displays, a series of nine each year, including those favourites of the Impressionists: orchids, nasturtiums, delphiniums and, of course, chrysanthemums. Between October and November each year dozens of varieties of chrysanthemums are used to create an explosion of colour and texture, based on the Japanese-style single stem. The museum gardeners use Japanese cultivation methods to achieve this, with each plant carefully pinched and pruned into a tall individual bloom during its growing period of June to October. These were the style of blooms seen in the painting by Bunker. A pink-tinged incurved chrysanthemum of the Japanese style has been named 'Isabella' in memory of her dedication to art and the chrysanthemum.

Fellow artist Mathias J. Alten (1871–1938) also included chrysanthemums among his flower paintings, although he is now primarily known for his land- and seascapes. Known as the Dean of Michigan Artists, German-born Alten produced nearly 3,800 paintings in his lifetime, 60 per cent of which were produced in Michigan. Never really adhering to a 'school', he travelled widely in France, Spain and America, including artists' colonies in Taos, New Mexico, and Old Lyme, Connecticut, and knew John Singer Sargent and Van Gogh. His most famous chrysanthemum canvas is filled with flowers seemingly collapsing on long stalks and appearing to imitate a spider or crane fly, while another depicts the large yellow and white blooms again falling under their own weight despite the support of an unusually tall jug or vase.

Both of these Alten paintings depict crooked and bent stalks and blooms almost at the end of their lives – a contrast with his sunny and vibrant outdoor scenes. Indeed chrysanthemums do seem to often bring out the alternative approach in artists. Piet Cornelis Mondrian (1872–1944) is best known for his large abstract geometric works in blocks of solid colour, but for more than a decade after leaving art school in 1897 Mondrian created naturalistic paintings and drawings, including more than 250 of flowers, often chrysanthemums. Usually portrayed as single stalks and heads against plain or obscured backgrounds, these concentrated observations are of what Mondrian described as the 'plastic structure' or essence of the flower itself: 'The depiction of the external as an approach to understanding the interior or deeper beauty and purpose.' 'I always confine myself to expressing the universal, that is, the eternal (closest to the spirit) and I do so in the simplest of external forms, in order to be able to express the inner meaning as lightly veiled as possible.'[8]

However, the style of Mondrian's depictions changes over the period from the late 1890s onwards, and according also to the medium he chose there are some clear influences. For example Vincent Van Gogh's *Dying Sunflowers* is echoed in Mondrian's *Dying Sunflower* as well as his alternative, *Dying Chrysanthemum*.

Mondrian appears to have chosen the chrysanthemum for multiple paintings due to a fascination with the complexity of its petal arrangement: his reaction to the orchid (which he never painted) was that it was only line with none of the bulky mass of the chrysanthemum and therefore not as interesting. He gave a wedding present of one of his many chrysanthemum paintings to the future Queen Wilhelmina of the Netherlands on her marriage in 1901 to Duke Henry of Mecklenburg-Schwerin, although as the ceremony took place in February, the wedding venue itself was decorated with orange blossom and white roses rather than chrysanthemums.

A study of Mondrian's chrysanthemum paintings on behalf of the Cleveland Museum of Art (who hold one of the more unusual paintings) has concluded that they may be divided into four periods, much as chrysanthemums themselves may be divided into several categories or types. His early 'Bouquet' period (*c.* 1897) shows clear similarities to works by nineteenth-century Impressionist artists such as Manet, Monet and Pissarro, while the 'Flat Frontal Flower' period or group (*c.* 1900s) appears to refer back to Japanese stylized prints or botanical art of the seventeenth century. So-called 'Expressionist Flowers' (1906–14) seem to form the longest-lasting period and include flowers other than chrysanthemums, most usually in singles and in all stages of bloom and senescence. Here the autumnal symbolism of the chrysanthemum appears in art form, sometimes appearing to drop and melt on the canvas, a microcosm of life, death and regeneration.[9]

In 1908 Mondrian experimented with anti-natural colour, with the famous blue-leafed chrysanthemum now in the Solomon R. Guggenheim Museum in New York. In his autobiographical essay in 1924 Mondrian reflected on this moment, recalling, 'the first thing to change in my painting was the colour. I forsook natural colour for pure colour. I had come to feel that the colours of nature cannot be reproduced on canvas.'[10]

The much later flower works by Mondrian mostly returned to softer, more commercially inspired forms, as the artist needed the income that these would provide, although gentle blues and rose colours still separate reality from nature. Recent studies have explained Mondrian's obsession with portraying the chrysanthemum as the 'feminine ideal' in his otherwise rectilinear world, the fulfilment and reflection of his inner life as an individual and a painter.[11]

While Monet and Caillebotte were planting chrysanthemums, and Piet Mondrian was experimenting with substituting 'pure colour for natural colour' in the chrysanthemum bloom, much of the rest of Europe and America were experiencing a Japanese craze which brought the flower to the attention of gardeners as well as artists. Interest in Japanese culture and design had started as early as the mid-nineteenth century, when the Museum of Ornamental Art, London (later to become the Victoria and Albert Museum) started to collect Japanese lacquer and porcelain works. In 1862 the

Piet Mondrian, *Chrysanthemum*, 1907. One of a series in which Mondrian sought to capture the 'essential being of the flower'.

International Exhibition in London had a Japanese section for the first time, considered to be one of the most influential events in the history of Japanese art in the West and coincidentally synchronizing with Robert Fortune's introduction of seven new Japanese chrysanthemums into England, including some with large heads and narrow, fantastical petals.[12]

By the 1880s *Japonisme* had become a specific style cult within the aesthetic movement, and gardens were at the forefront of this, with books such as Josiah Conder's *Landscape Gardening in Japan* (1893) fanning the craze. Japanese displays became an expected part of the series of international exhibitions taking place in England and France through the 1880s and '90s, culminating in the dedicated 'Japan-British Exhibition' of 1910 at White City, London. That most famous of Gilbert and Sullivan operettas, *The Mikado*, was the success of the season in 1885 on both sides of the Atlantic, and with its lure of silk kimonos and heavily painted women, the Anglo-Japanese theme was one that theatres, and chrysanthemum growers, were loathe to give up.

The writers Arthur Anderson and Leedham Bantock were undoubtedly hoping to repeat the success of *The Mikado* when they penned *The White Chrysanthemum* (1905). This light-hearted musical in three acts boasted a full panoply of delightful young women, confused suitors, irascible fathers and American heiresses. Setting the work in Japan allowed the heroine (Sybil) to spend much of the play in an inauthentic mix of silk and chiffon, heavily embroidered with storks, dragons and chrysanthemums. The implausible story revolved around the romance between Sybil and her suitor Reggie Cunningham, who travelled to Japan to be together and once there lived a life of chastity awaiting permission from Reggie's father for their marriage. Reggie's father has other ideas, wanting Reggie to marry Cornelia Vanderdecken, a wealthy American heiress – a common enough event at a time when wealthy American women were said to predatorily haunt the London season on the lookout for poverty-stricken aristocrats in need of a wife. Less common was the arrival of father and prospective American wife in Japan, as happens in *The White Chrysanthemum*. The arrival results in the hasty disguising of Sybil, who from this point onwards in the play wore only white silk clothing and clutched a white chrysanthemum to her bosom or her lips, depending on the scene. Whether this pose was an added 'disguise' or done to enable Reggie to distinguish her from the Japanese maids and servants was not made clear.

The most successful song in the show was that sung by Sybil's maid Betty and her mistress and was titled, of course, 'White Chrysanthemum'. Sybil, and her 'alter ego' O'San, was originally played by the popular opera singer and actress Isabel Jay (1879–1927), who in the promotional shots bore at least some slight resemblance to a Japanese woman, with her dark hair and petite looks. It was, however, the various changes of costume, rather than the storyline, that attracted most attention, with reviews in both the stage press and fashion magazines commenting on the white silks and the embroidered 'chrysanthemums in full bloom'. Although one fashion review commented that 'Her kimono of white satin and gold embroidery, though a very becoming garment, is not exactly true to Japanese fashion,' before concluding wisely that with regard to cultural exactitude 'one must not be too critical in musical comedy.'

Isabel Jay had worked for Gilbert and Sullivan's D'Oyly Carte Opera Company earlier in her career, including playing Yum-Yum in *The Mikado*, which was still immensely popular when she appeared in it in the late 1890s. *The White Chrysanthemum* was not to be as long-lasting, closing in London's West End in 1906 after a very creditable 197 performances. Jay retired from the stage in 1911 having gone on to play an international assortment of characters, including a Balkan princess, Miss Hook of Holland and a princess from the mythical country of Cadonia, as well as the rather more humdrum Olivia in a musical adaptation of Oliver Goldsmith's *The Vicar of Wakefield*, with no chrysanthemums to hide behind.

Rather than being actresses, exotic geishas or opera singers, the two women who did most to popularize the chrysanthemum in

"MIKADO" Chrysanthemums.
xxx SET OF xxx

The Chrysanthemums named on this page are the choicest productions from all exhibitions and sources for the year 1898. Our patrons can rely on them being each and every one the very choicest color, as awards are not given until the judges are satisfied that they are better than any existing sorts. So, if you wish to be up to date, and have the very best, order this set. IN ORDERING SAY "MIKADO SET."

PRICE, 10 CENTS EACH; THE SET OF TEN FOR 50 CENTS: ANY FIVE FOR 25 CENTS.

LORNA DOONE.
This variety is of mammoth size, purest snow-white in color, very broad, heavy, deep flower, measuring fourteen inches in diameter. When the flower is several days old the outer petals curl and interlace. Probably the largest of all whites, and no doubt the very best. This charming variety has taken prizes wherever shown. It is as pure in color as it namesake was in character in Blackmore's beautiful romance.

SUNDEW.
n exhibition bronze. The flower is of immense size, crowded with petals which are stiff and of great substance. Form incurving, depth about three and one-half inches. A most imposing bloom. Color Indian-red, faced with bronze. Received $50 premium at Indianapolis as best bronze.

BELLE OF CASTLEWOOD.
One of the grandest varieties of the year. Flowers of immense size, almost spherical, outer petals recurving slightly, quite double, and carried on a good stem. The color is a soft lemon, suffused with pink. This is the variety that took the silver cup at Madison Square, offered for the best pink.

HER MAJESTY.
The sensational variety of the year. It has won prizes and certificates everywhere shown. It is an enormous globular Japanese, with broad, incurving petals. Color white, shading to pale lemon. The flowers are often twelve inches in diameter. It is undoubtedly the most meritorious variety of the year.

DEFENDER.
This is the richest deep crimson variety we have ever seen, and excels in its color. The color is of the richest, velvety-crimson, which in the flower itself is soft and velvety-like. The outer petals are broad and drooping, and have a lustrous sheen in the sunlight. The form is flat, with drooping outer petals, which gives it a very graceful appearance.

GOLDEN TROPHY.
The largest yellow in existence. This magnificent new Chrysanthemum was exhibited last Fall, measuring over fifteen inches in diameter, and is, without exception, the largest yellow Chrysanthemum ever introduced. The color is deep, rich yellow, the half-expanded flower incurving. Some idea of the value of the new sort may be formed from the fact that the introducer had the entire stock sold one year in advance. The flowers are of enormous size. We have no hesitancy in saying that we regard this the best of all yellow Chrysanthemums.

MARQUIS MORTEMARTE.
A superb, clear Mermet rose-pink, petals thick and heavy, cup-shaped, solid to the center, immense in size, having been exhibited eleven inches across. The best pink in commerce. Awarded silver medal by Pennsylvania Horticultural Society.

SUNSTONE.
Petals hook up at the end, showing the light straw reverse; upper surface bright yellow, shading to red at the base. The flower being flat, shows the three colors to advantage. The most beautiful combination of colors yet produced. Seven inches in diameter. Awarded first-class certificate by the National Chrysanthemum Show, England.

JOHN SHRIMPTON.
Incurved Japanese bloom of large size and high-built, solid form. Deepest crimson, nearest approach to black. Never burns as crimsons are apt to do. Strong, healthy habit. Winner of silver cup at Madison Square Garden. 1895.

WESTERN KING.
In the entire Chrysanthemum family there is no grander white variety, no matter when it blooms. It is the most popular style, immense, incurving, broad, channeled petals, of great substance and the purest white. A perfect ball of snow. Sixteen to eighteen inches in circumference. We think this variety does not possess a single fault.

"Ostrich Plume" Set of Chrysanthemums.
PRICE, 10 CENTS EACH.

New White "Ostrich Plume," Mrs. Alpheus Hardy. The flowers are very large and of thick substance, perfect shape, and belong to the incurved Japanese section, while the color is the purest white. It is of immense size, broad petals and incurved, the surface being downy, like loose-piled plush. The entire flower seems frosted with glittering white. Its unique character consists in its fine, downy appearance, which is produced by the glandular hairs which cover the petals, which has been frequently described by the press as producing a fluffy effect, similar to an ostrich feather. It has received the highest honors wherever exhibited.

New Sweet-Scented "Ostrich Plume." Miss Anna Manda. Flower very high and compact, perfectly double, incurved, of the purest white. The numerous petals are well furnished with long, glandular, hair-like out-growths, giving the flower a unique appearance, far surpassing in attractiveness the celebrated Mrs. Alpheus Hardy. The plant is of strong and vigorous habit, carrying the flower erect on a stout stem. Another great

recommendation of this new variety is that the flower is sweet-scented.

New Yellow "Ostrich Plume," Gold Dust. A grand yellow, incurved, hairy variety of the "Ostrich Plume" class. The flowers are large, of a beautiful, clear golden-yellow, incurved, and covered with golden-yellow hairs. The plant is vigorous in growth, and the flower is borne upright on a stout stem. No collection can afford to be without this variety.

New Rosy-blush "Ostrich Plume." William Falconer. The color is an exquisite shade of rosy-blush, changing to a delicate flesh-pink as the flowers advance in age. A description can not convey the beauty of coloring found in this new variety. The delicacy of tinting is unsurpassed in any class of flowers within our knowledge. The soft, feathery growth peculiar to the "Ostrich Plume" class is pronounced, the effect being as if a soft-tinted, lace-like web or veil was thrown over the blooms, a unique and beautiful addition to its appearance. The flowers are of the largest size, and are borne on strong, vigorous stalks. The growth of the plant is all that could be desired.

SPECIAL OFFER.—The ten Mikado Set and the four Ostrich Plume Set of Chrysanthemums for 75 cents.

The operetta *The Mikado* inspired music lovers and chrysanthemum nurseries alike, as here in an American advertisement of 1899.

Miss Isabel Jay
(1879–1927)
in her role as Sybil
Cunningham, *The
White Chrysanthemum*.

England in the Edwardian period were 'Essex girls' who enjoyed nothing more risqué than painting and independent travel. Ella and Florence Du Cane were actually born in Hobart, Tasmania (Florence in 1869 and Ella in 1874), but the family was English; the girls returned to their home in Braxted, Essex, after their father's period as governor of Tasmania was over in 1875. The family had an interest in plants, perhaps due to their travels, and created gardens both at Braxted and their later home, called 'Mountains', also in Essex. Ella Du Cane taught herself to paint and in 1893, through the influence of a family friend, had a picture accepted at an exhibition of the Society of Painters in Water Colours. Gardens were her preferred subject, including those at Holland House (London), Chatsworth

Traditional Kimono fabric with abstract chrysanthemum motifs.

(Derbyshire), Hinchingbrooke House (Huntingdonshire) and Drummond Castle (Ireland), and in 1896 she painted the royal gardens at Frogmore, Windsor (Berkshire) and Osborne (Isle of Wight) for Queen Victoria. In 1898 an exhibition of 57 watercolours was patronized by the royal family, who went on to purchase several of them. However, the chrysanthemum link came not through these projects (although notably both Holland House and Hinchingbrooke had Japanese gardens), but through the sisters' travels abroad.

Travelling with her sister or the family, Florence once commented that before 1914 she had not spent a winter in Britain for twenty years. These travels included Madeira, Italy, Algiers, the Caribbean and, most notably, by 1904 Ceylon and Japan. A 1904 exhibition of her works included 'about a hundred paintings of flower-bright Japan'.[13] After a series of commissions to illustrate travel and flower books (including John Finnemore's *Japan* (1907)), Ella and Florence returned to Japan themselves to record more garden scenes. The result was over a hundred paintings exhibited at the Fine Art Gallery in London in 1908 (some purchased by Edward VII), plus the book *The Flowers and Gardens of Japan*, published in the same year. Rather than being a technical work, the authors included 'the flower legends and fairy tales, which are household words in every Japanese home' and the attractive combination of paintings and light text written by the travellers themselves gave this a broad appeal for both gardeners and armchair travellers, in a way which some of the more serious books on Japanese gardens, such as Josiah Conder's *Landscape Gardening in Japan*, had not.

After an initial introduction into the history of the Japanese garden in its homeland, its style and ornamental components (tea temples and so forth), the Du Cane sisters concentrated on the particular plants of Japanese gardens and tea gardens, including chapters on the peach, plum, cherry blossom, wisteria, azalea, iris, lotus, bamboo and, naturally, the chrysanthemum.[14] They rehearsed the story of the chrysanthemum as an imperial emblem, with the additional note that at the time of the Du Cane sisters' travels the current emperor had his birthday in the month of the chrysanthemum (November), making this connection even more apt. This imperial connection may account for the fact that the best-known chrysanthemum raisers during the period of the sisters' travels were the aristocrats Count Okuma and Count Sakai, both of whom apparently spent much of their fortunes on their plants – a habit which the Du Cane sisters decried, being proponents of lavishing 'time and care' rather than money. They also decried the artificiality of the great Japanese chrysanthemum show held at Dangozaka, quoting in translation the poet Hoichi Shonin, who was said to have written: 'What an inferior heart of man; Lo! A waxwork chrysanthemum show!'[15] Although one has to wonder if something more spiritual had been lost in translation.

The sisters spent several months in Japan, enabling them to record the preparation for these shows, starting with the tying in of buds to skeleton frames that would later form dresses or figures. The show at Dangozaka was not without a contemporary note: a few years prior to the sisters' visit the Russo-Japanese War (1904–5) had apparently been reflected in the scenes depicted in the complex chrysanthemum tableaux, including a representation of the blocking of the harbour at Port Arthur, with Captain Hiroze and his fellow *keshitai* (translated as 'those determined to die') as the characters.[16] The scene had been composed of 2,000 chrysanthemum plants featuring a sea of dark-coloured flowers with white crests. A further scene represented the Russian admiral Makaroff, who was shown standing on the bridge of his ship, sword in hand, as the boat sank below the flowery waves. Despite being an enemy, such a show of stalwart sacrifice was admired by the Japanese and regarded worthy of floral tribute. According to the Du Cane sisters, the scene was remembered for its 'veritable storm of white flowers, dashed with red, and here and there a few sailors groping blindly'.[17] The dramatic quality of these scenes was repeated in a representation of the night after the great battle of Lia Yang (Liaoyang, 1904), when the spirits of the dead soldiers were depicted flower-clad with white swords in their hands.

Alongside dramatic scenes such as this were the traditional showman's plants, exquisitely arranged to show off their blooms. The sisters were enchanted by the poetic quality of the names, translating them as 'The Sky at Dawn' (*Ake-no-sora*), 'Waves in the Morning Sun' (*Asa hi no nami*), 'Companions of the Moon' (*Tsuki-no-tomo*) and

'Shadows of the Evening Moon' (*Yu hi kage*). All these were of appropriate colours with dawn a pale pink, the morning sun waving in pale red, the evening sun setting dull red and the lunar companions white. The 'Princesses of the Blood' stood in resplendent graceful rows of flower-heads 'as white as the driven snow', referring presumably to the virginal purity of the princesses themselves, rather than the blood of their imperial line.[18] This aristocratic flower contrasted with the tale of a modern chrysanthemum grower that the Du Canes visited. Led by a mutual acquaintance through the 'whole length and breadth of the fish market', the stallholder they eventually met revealed a secret courtyard garden of lanterns, bamboo, shrines and chrysanthemums hidden behind the more mundane world of raw fish. In this secret court the blossoms 'seemed to represent every colour, shape and size that it was possible for a chrysanthemum to assume, all perfectly grown plants', including rarities of which there were 'only two other plants of the same kind in Japan'.[19] Labels adorning some of the plants indicated that they had been chosen by the emperor himself to be sent from the humble fishmonger to adorn the Imperial collection.

The chrysanthemum-growing fishmonger appealed to Florence Du Cane (the writer of the text of *The Flowers and Gardens of Japan*, her sister being the artist) as an example of how a humble but diligent worker may attain the same perfection as the wealthy but indigent aristocrat. This moral tale, included in detail in their book, pandered to the then English fashion for dividing the deserving worker from the undeserving idler – although where the wealthy world-travelling Du Canes placed themselves along this spectrum is a matter of conjecture. The Japanese system of personal sacrifice for the greater good (most especially for one's own descendants) was also on display as Florence went on to explain that despite being seemingly in their prime, the flowers were all to be cut down the following day to secure the best cuttings for the following year's plants.

Several other legends about the chrysanthemum were recounted to the Du Canes and through them to the English reader, passed on

The books and paintings of Ella and Florence Du Cane encouraged the creation of 'Japanese' gardens in England.

with more or less empathy in their text. The traditional Japanese tale of Soeman Akana, the sick man tended by Samon Hase, who promises to return again on the 'day of the chrysanthemum feast' and stay the rest of his days with his new 'friend and brother' ends with Soeman killing himself in prison on the eve of the appointed day so that his

spirit may fly to keep his appointment. 'I rode on the wind to see you on this day of my chrysanthemum promise,' says the spirit at the end of this tale of great love, and of the traditional Japanese respect for promises given and debts owed. Only to be followed by Florence Du Cane's observation that 'if this legend were taught in the schools of to-day a moral might be pointed with advantages on the subject of keeping appointments and promises' – a comment that seems to rather miss the point of the tale.

The chapter in *The Flowers and Gardens of Japan* on the modern-day shows and ancient legends of the chrysanthemum was accompanied by three illustrations by Ella Du Cane of chrysanthemums in Japanese gardens, each exquisite watercolour evoking the style of a Japanese garden and the colour of the chrysanthemums grown there. Although the book was not as well received as some of their others, being criticized by the *Evening Standard* for not displaying 'the special palette . . . of the country', it sold well and was popular both with gardeners and plant collectors as well as those who wanted to gain a general impression of Japan. It sold especially well during the 'Japan-British Exhibition' of 1910 and some of the illustrations, including the chrysanthemum gardens, were reproduced as postcards by the Raphael Tuck company and sold as souvenirs of the exhibition.

After their travels to Japan, the sisters' next projects were *The Flowers and Gardens of Madeira* (1908), *The Canary Islands* (1911) and a more general work, *On the Banks of the Nile*, in 1913, a journey that Florence later said was taken much against the personal advice of Lord Kitchener. During the First World War Florence went to France and ran a hospital for La Croix-Rouge (the French Red Cross), twice being captured by the Germans. She was awarded the Croix de Guerre by the French general Ferdinand Foch personally for her bravery. Ella, however, disappeared from the public eye, and as the fashion for travel books was not regained after 1918, no more publications and associated tours were embarked upon by the sisters.[20] Florence returned to

Tea temples such as the ones illustrated by the Du Cane sisters could be purchased in Liberty of London.

Travel to Japan and China became popular in the early 20th century.

their mother's home in Essex and embarked on a career in garden design, while Ella 'retired' to nearby Beacon Hill House, where she too gardened and of course painted the results of her efforts.

The sisters' time in Japan obviously influenced Florence, as a 1925 article in *Country Life* on the Du Cane family house and garden at 'Mountains' (Essex) includes a description of 'One of the earliest Japanese Gardens in Britain by Lady Du Cane, which still exists by the stream in the garden'.[21] Japanese irises from the nursery of Hori-Kiri and a Japanese thatched tea-house were also present, and one hopes some chrysanthemums, although as the article was written in March there is no comment on the beauties of the imperial autumnal flower.

The exhibition that the Raphael Tuck postcards by Ella Du Cane were advertising, and which acted as such as promotion for *The Flowers and Gardens of Japan*, was the 'Japan-British Exhibition' of 1910 (sometimes referred to as the Anglo-Japanese Exhibition). One of several Japanese exhibitions of the early nineteenth century, this was driven by Japan's desire to improve public relations and encourage tourism following the renewal of the Anglo-Japanese Alliance. Based at White

City in London, it was the largest foreign exposition that the empire of Japan had ever participated in and lasted over five months. There were more than 2,000 exhibitors of arts, crafts and technology housed alongside two large Japanese gardens complete with tea tents where the famous tea ceremony was enacted, as well as a Japanese naval cruiser docked at Gravesend in Kent.

These gardens were designed as authentic Japanese gardens rather than the hybrid Anglo-Japanese style that had already infiltrated both England and France, and they were constructed from scratch at the exhibition site. Trees, shrubs, wooden buildings, bridges, and even stones, were brought in from Japan as well as the actual designers and gardeners. The two gardens were named the Garden of the Floating Isle (replete with Japanese tea-house) and the Garden of Peace. Although not rich in flowers, instead focusing on the 'architectural' elements and layout of a traditional Japanese garden, they gave further impetus to quasi-Japanese gardens and planting in England. Visited by 8 million people between 14 May and 29 October, they gave a boost to the popularity of plants such as the orchid, bamboo and chrysanthemum, all of which began to appear in even the most 'popular' of gardening books. In 1911 the *Chokushi-Mon* (Gateway of the Imperial Messenger) from the exhibition was moved to Kew Gardens, where its stylized flower and animal carving can still be seen, including of course the chrysanthemum emblem.

Also at Kew at that date was a chrysanthemum house, images of which can still be seen on historic postcards, although the official histories of Kew are strangely quiet about its existence. Records indicate that the similar house at Roath Park gardens, Cardiff, set up in 1907, was sent chrysanthemums from Kew to assist its own inauguration. Specialist chrysanthemum houses also existed at Battersea Park in London and Liverpool Botanic Gardens, the latter of which also hosted a Chrysanthemum Show. The glory of these 'cool' chrysanthemum houses in public parks and botanic gardens around the country is now more often recorded in faded postcards than modern guidebooks and few, if any, appear to survive in their original guise.

One of many long-lost chrysanthemum houses at botanic gardens — the one at Kew has even disappeared from popular histories.

It was at Kew that the botanical artist Marianne North (1830–1890) first became obsessed with exotic plants, thanks to her friendship with the then director William Hooker. Best known for her subsequent intrepid travels around the world, Marianne painted the new 'Japanese' chrysanthemums in the comfort of her own home in England. Like most women of the period she had originally taken up floral watercolour painting as a hobby. This was an accomplishment widely approved of by society in general and specifically by the influential writer John Claudius Loudon, who stated in the *Gardener's Magazine* of 1831 that

> to be able to draw flowers botanically and fruit horticulturally, that is with the characteristics by which varieties and sub-varieties are distinguished, is one of the most useful accomplishments of young ladies of leisure living in the country.[22]

Loudon did not specify which plants it was best to paint, although female artists were expected to shy away from anything with overt sexual parts, preferring the shy violet to the sexy hibiscus. The chry-santhemum, with its bright colours and strong petals, would not usually have been a favoured subject of delicate ladies of leisure but Marianne North was made of sterner stuff even before she started her world travels. Her family's social contacts had put her in touch with William and Joseph Hooker at Kew Gardens, each in turn director of that burgeoning botanic garden, and she had started to explore the wonders of the botanical world in all their detail.

Marianne's switch to oils from watercolours, brought on by a visit from the Australian artist Robert Hawker Dowling, coincided with the new fashion for Japanese chrysanthemums and produced some of the most striking early English depictions of them. She described painting in oils as 'an addiction, like dram drinking', adding: 'I have never done anything else since as being once taken up it is almost impossible to leave up once it has possession of one.'[23] As Marianne's paintings of the Japanese chrysanthemums demonstrate, oils suited her style and allowed her to depict the strong colours and shapes she adored. The vibrant chrysanthemums may also have influenced her in her decision to travel the world in search of more intensely coloured flowers, this time to be painted in their own exotic countries. Her paintings are now housed in a gallery at Kew paid for by Marianne herself.

Pure white chrysanthemums were nurtured in John Steinbeck's short story 'The Chrysanthemums' (1937).

six

A Literary Bouquet

❦

Nothing in the history of the chrysanthemum prepared the world for John Steinbeck's use of the flower as a cry for women's equality. Published in *Harper's Magazine* in October 1937, Steinbeck's short story 'The Chrysanthemums' captured a moment in America's history between the Great Depression of the late 1920s and 1930s, a harsh period of dust-bowl conditions and high male unemployment, with accompanying inequalities, and the slow rise of equality and liberation for women with the recovering economy. Steinbeck's 'heroine', Elisa Allen, has become a symbol of the downtrodden women in 1930s America. She is introduced to readers as a strong and capable woman trapped in the domain of household and garden. Her clothes and appearance suffer no appeals to femininity or frippery, and her role and attitudes appear to conflict even with the womanly role to which her marriage and husband tie her. Weary of her life and bored with her husband, the only hint of an outlet for her emotional and physical abilities is the care she pours into tending her beloved chrysanthemums; their short-livedness is emphasized by the tinker who describes them as like 'a quick puff of coloured smoke'.[1] It is while she is cutting the deadheads off the chrysanthemums and feeling for new growth at their bases, with no snails or sowbugs or cutworms, that the story commences, Elisa herself framed between the oppressive but solid past and the fragile shoots of the future.

It is a nomadic tinker who intrudes into the brusque and hard-edged world that surrounds Elisa, with its 'hard-swept' and 'hard-polished' surfaces. Offering a glimpse of the world beyond and a supposedly shared (although actually false) love of the chrysanthemums that Elisa has fixed her emotional life around, the tinker offers to mend the pots and pans of the household and perhaps holds out the hope of mending Elisa's life. In exchange, she gifts him her precious seedlings, sharing her one personal and private joy with this complete stranger who has penetrated to the heart of her love for these ephemeral beauties with their powder-puff appearance in glorious whites and yellows.

Elisa's transformation while she shares secrets that will procure for a stranger the exuberantly large chrysanthemum is complete. Ripping off her masculine gloves and hat, she lets loose her long hair, urges the tinker to enter her garden and describes both the practical and intuitive, almost sexual, care of the tender, young green buds. The tinker responds with 'secrets' of his own, revealing emotional but cunning depths as he exchanges a professed response to the natural world for Elisa's offer of a more practical paid task. As the tinker leaves in his cart with the precious burden of chrysanthemum shoots, Elisa's inner and outer life are briefly transformed and she changes into a dress, applying make-up and her best underclothes in preparation for an evening on the town with her husband, a delight previously scorned. Standing on the border between masculine and feminine, Elisa longs for a new life just as the chrysanthemums reinvent themselves each year, while her husband merely responds that she looks 'strong enough to break a calf over her knee and happy enough to eat it like a watermelon'.

The denouement comes as the newly happy Elisa, bolstered by the stranger's appreciation of her abilities, sights the fragile flowers cast away by the side of the road. Having relinquished (within a few hundred words and one short day) her original role as the de facto head of the household, with her masculine clothes and shoes, for a strong female role marked by success and the thriving chrysanthemums, Elisa

Brightly coloured chrysanthemums bring cheer to the heart.

is now reduced to the traditional role of the weak emotional female. As easily crushed underfoot as the delicate petals, the strength she felt only hours ago is gone,[2] and, in the words of Steinbeck 'she has become an old woman.'[3] Although it is impossible to know whether or not Steinbeck ever saw it, Fannie Eliza Duval's painting *Chrysanthemum Garden California* (1891) could stand exactly for the garden of Elisa, with a strong woman in grey clothing and practical hat tending blazing white chrysanthemums in a landscape where everything else appears hazy and indistinct.

With its background in the Salinas Valley, California, Steinbeck's story of small farmers struggling to survive against the vagaries of climate focuses on the equivocal role of childless women such as Elisa, strong enough to act in a male world but not allowed to do so fully, while unable to maintain a femininity in the face of day-to-day needs. With her nurturing and 'procreative' hands and soul trodden on by her marriage and duties as well as by the tinker, Elisa is eventually left with neither strength nor femininity. Even her innate ability to grow plants, referred to by her husband as so remarkable as to be a magical 'gift', will perhaps desert her now it has been shared with a stranger, and the next season's chrysanthemums may not grow to the 'monstrous proportion' of those that had flowered in this year's garden.

Fecundity and sterility, femininity and masculinity, equality and inequality, sexuality and sterility, betrayal and hope – all are encapsulated in Steinbeck's masterpiece, along with echoes of the Garden of Eden forever spoiled as husband and wife depart the tight boundaries of their garden and orchard for the dubious joys of the town, with its fancy food and wine, and the possibility of fights so bloody 'the gloves become heavy and soggy with blood', echoing the soiled gardening gloves that Elisa was wearing when the story opened. It is, however, the chrysanthemums which form the focus of the story, with their odd combination of strength and fragility, death and rebirth, and inability to seed themselves, a perfect metaphor for Elisa – the childless woman crushed by a world that has no role that fulfils her nature. 'The Chrysanthemums' has formed a core text in studies of twentieth-century American literature in the decades since its original publication, and has been constantly interpreted and reinterpreted in the context of a changing society as well as providing greater understanding of the culture of the 1930s. In 1990 it was even made into a 23-minute film by Steve Rosen and Nina Capriola for Pyramid Film and Video of Santa Monica.

In fact, the chrysanthemum as a bright hope in a downtrodden life appeared in another short story, by the New Zealand writer

Katherine Mansfield, decades before Steinbeck's iconic work, although the settings are very different.[4] In 'The Singing Lesson' (1920) Mansfield introduces her reader to the icy despair and hatred of a music mistress whose engagement and hopes of marriage have been cruelly ended with a letter. Clutching the pain to herself like a knife, Miss Meadows – 'pierced to the heart' – leads her young charges in the mournful lament: 'Fast! Ah, too fast fade the roses of pleasure; soon autumn yields unto winter drear.' With the autumn of her life seemingly frozen now to inevitable winter (Miss Meadows is thirty in the tale; her erstwhile beau, Basil, 25), she cruelly refuses the habitual offer of a 'beautiful yellow chrysanthemum' from an eager pupil, thus inflicting on the young Mary Beazley the same pain that she herself is feeling.

With its associations of sunshine after summer's end, the flower seems to mock the newly spurned schoolmistress in the same way as the cast-aside seedlings mocked Elisa in Steinbeck's story. For Miss Meadows, however, there is to be a happy ending, as a telegram arrives from the seemingly indecisive Basil and, called away from her class to receive it, Miss Meadows learns that fate has not after all reserved spinsterhood for her, however loveless the eventual match might be. As she returns to instruct the class to sing 'flowers o'erladen' and 'baskets of fruit and ribbons to boot', Miss Meadows reprieves the chrysanthemum, using its sunshine petals to hide a smile – perhaps of happiness, perhaps of triumph – as both the character and the reader realize that it is the match not the man that is her aim. Some might see the late-flowering chrysanthemum as heavy-handed symbolism in this short story, which has few of the subtleties of Steinbeck, but the intensity of the bright yellow masking Basil's own confessions of disgust regarding the prospective marriage brings a brittle artificiality to the supposed happy ending.[5]

D. H. Lawrence's short story 'Odour of Chrysanthemums' also chooses the single flower and an individual woman character as a focus.[6] The chrysanthemums here are not the blazing large white blooms of the Salinas Valley but instead small, fragile and pink, almost wild as a daisy. Written in 1909 and published two years later, in this story the chrysanthemums of the title mark the passages of life and eventual death. The male character, Walter Bates, is late coming home one day and his wife Elizabeth after a while goes to find him, only to discover that he is dead as the result of an accident. Looking back over her marriage, the chrysanthemums seem to appear at every junction in the relationship that is now over: 'It was chrysanthemums when I married him, and chrysanthemums when you were born, and the first time they ever brought him home drunk, he'd got brown chrysanthemums in his coat.'[7]

It was this short story, set against the harsh life of the colliery and the tragedy of a mining accident, that was to set Lawrence on the path to fame, as it was sent for possible publication to Ford Madox Ford, then editor of the *English Review*. Madox Ford later recalled:

I was reading in the twilight in the long eighteenth-century room that was at once the office of the *English Review* and my drawing-room. My eyes were tired; I had been reading all day so I did not go any further with the story. It was called *Odour of Chrysanthemums*. I laid it in the basket for accepted manuscripts. My secretary looked up and said: 'You've got another genius?' I answered: 'It's a big one this time,' and went upstairs to dress.[8]

In 'Odour of Chrysanthemums' it is the increasing coarseness of her husband that has turned Elizabeth away from him during his life and even after death, contrasting with the unusually frail chrysanthemum flowers that appear at turning points in their lives. More predictably, large autumnal chrysanthemums appear as metaphor in the 'coming of old-age' novel *The Chrysanthemum Garden* by Joseph Cowley (1981). Themes of late blossoming infuse the story as the central character, again a woman, feels emotionally and intellectually divorced from her thick-hided chauvinist husband. Breaking away to find a new outlet for her creative nature, Morna attends poetry classes, where she finds common ground with the accomplished and acclaimed poet Denison McArdle (Denny), now in his seventies but still 'America's foremost poet'.

Acknowledging that theirs is a love that will carry them through years of ageing and death, Morna and Denny embark on an affair that transforms the soft autumn of their lives into brilliant blossom. In the story, the chrysanthemum garden of the title was planted by Morna in the lovers' New Hampshire home in the knowledge that the flowers would 'blossom in the fall after everything else had died, large red and pink and purple and white blossoms that would contrast with the brown, dying leaves of the trees'; in the same way that their love would blossom and she (in her fifties) and Denny (in his seventies) aged and eventually passed from their world. Indeed the chrysanthemums were flowering in their autumnal yellow, red and purple blossoms, 'backdropped by frosted weeds' and iced puddles on the day that Denny had the massive stroke that led to his death three days later. Unlike Steinbeck's chrysanthemums, these flowers represented love fulfilled in the autumn of life rather than the stifling emotional death of Elisa, but still they combine their majestic blooms with a poignant sadness that purveys the story and the changing season, and again death haunts this flower associated with change in both Eastern and Western cultures.[9]

Motifs of age and the triumph of intellectual beauty over coarseness leap both time and cultures to link *The Chrysanthemum Garden* and 'The Chrysanthemums' with the trilogy of stories by the writer Fumiko Hayashi (1903–1951), comprising 'Bangiku' (1948), 'Shirosagi' (1949) and 'Suisen' (1949). These were written during the 'golden age' of Japanese short stories (*c.* 1905–48) when Western culture and Japanese tradition blended in literature. Themes centre on balancing the more traditional culture, where nature was seen as a force for good, with the need for adaptation to a modern world.

The focus of the film trilogy is three retired geishas, Kin, Tamae and Tomi, trying to make ends meet in post-war Japan, and the story is one that blends changes in life with the changing of life's seasons so that the chrysanthemum theme refers both to the women and their journey in life, as well as the history of their 'decorative' role'. Kin has married a money-lender and wrapped herself in layers of uncaring that slowly unpeel as she rejects first him, and then her former lovers Tabe and Seki, who in turn attempt to persuade her back for their own monetary advantages. Trained all her life to care for beauty within and around her, but aware of her perilous position as an ageing woman in the harsh post-war period, Kin eventually turns her back on all the men and sets out to make a new life for herself, leaving the inebriated (and indebted to her) Tamae behind.

Fumiko Hayashi, the writer of the story, had moved to Tokyo with a lover and lived with several men until marrying the painter Rokubin Tezuka in 1926; and many of her works revolve around themes of free-spirited women and troubled relationships. She classed herself as a 'wanderer', travelling to Java and Sumatra as well as in occupied Japan, and is now thought of as an early feminist. One feels that she would have had much sympathy for Steinbeck's downtrodden Elisa if she had lived long enough to read his 'version' of the chrysanthemum tale. In 1954 the Japanese film-maker Mikio Naruse turned Hayashi's three stories into a film using the title *Late Chrysanthemums*, based on the name of the first of the trilogy – *Bangiku* – making what was widely considered 'his most perfect film', with starring roles for the three geishas, as rarely seen in cinema as in real life.

In sharp contrast to the proto-feminist Elisa and indeed the age-ing Japanese geisha, is the rather pampered 'society woman' and chrysanthemum grower in Saki's 'The Stalled Ox'. Written by the witty satirical writer Hector Hugh Munro (1870–1916), who took the pen-name 'Saki', the short story takes place, as did so many of his works, in a usually peaceful Edwardian villa (and gardens) during the years preceding the First World War. His characters, often aspiring and culturally and socially pretentious, are observed with great detail and wit although not without sympathy. Theophil Eshley, the 'hero' of the piece, is 'an artist by profession and a cattle painter by force of environment', living in a 'park-like villa that only just escaped the reproach of being suburban' and conveniently situated close to fields and meadows where drowsy cattle lived out their picturesque lives.[10]

One quiet afternoon his painting reverie is interrupted by the wild knockings of a neighbour, who announces that an ox has found its way into her garden, where it is creating havoc: the garden being small and the ox large and hungry. Mistaking Eshley's tendency to paint cows for a knowledge of cattle in general and oxen in particular, Adela Pingsford believes that he is the man to come to her aid. On their return to the garden Adela Pingsford and the unfortunate and reluctant Eshley find the ox singling out Adela's chrysanthemums for its particular digestive enjoyment, the scene being set in 'late autumn'. With typically understated humour Saki details the increasingly icy exchanges between the irate Adela and the flummoxed artist called on to evict the ox with nothing better than a pea stick as a weapon. Eventually the animal lumbers into the house via the French windows to continue its munching on vases of flowers. With nothing else to do Eshley grabs easel and palette and commences on a fine painting, later to be entitled *Ox in a Morning Room: Late Autumn*.

This painting revolutionizes his career and the quiet pastoral paintings of drowsy cattle are a thing of the past, with *Barbary Apes Wrecking a Boudoir* following two years later. It is the careful observance of the characters and their pretensions that provides much of the humour. The ox traverses a 'tiny strip of turf that the charitable called the croquet lawn' in order to gain entrance to the house, while the chrysanthemums it disposes of are not mere flowers but, as Adela Pingsford takes care to point out even at this most critical of moments, include the glowing orange head of a 'Mademoiselle Louise Bichot'. Eshley replies that as she has been so frank as to the variety of chrysanthemum he is happy to inform her that it is an Ayrshire Ox who has seen to its demise, along with almost all of its companions, both in the garden and in vases about the morning room. Originally published in 1914 in a short story collection titled *Beasts and Superbeasts*, Saki's story is so well known that today an online search for the chrysanthemum 'Mademoiselle Louise Bichot' inevitably turns

At the time
he stole the
plum-coloured
chrysanthemums,
Beverley Nichols
lived in a cottage
in the village
of Glatton,
Huntingdonshire,
which he
immortalized
as 'Allways'.

up the Saki short story; and so it has become nearly impossible to discover whether there ever was a person of the name of Mademoiselle Louise Bichot or indeed a chrysanthemum named after her.[11]

It was the temptations of rare chrysanthemums in the chrysanthemum house at Kew which was to be the downfall of the garden writer Beverley Nichols (1898–1983). Garden writers rarely get into trouble for the flights of fantasy that fall from their pens but Beverley Nichols's chrysanthemum story resulted in a brisk telling off by the director of the Royal Botanic Gardens. Best known for his humorous gardening tales, mixed with the occasional (some would say very occasional) piece of horticultural advice, Nichols wrote a series of books based on his own gardens in Surrey and Huntingdonshire. He also wrote short articles for less practical garden periodicals, where his 'poetic' and tongue-in-cheek style sat well with the often slightly snobbish approach to the garden.

It was just such an article in the magazine *My Garden* which caused the chrysanthemum-related ruckus. *My Garden* was founded and edited by Theo Stephens and aimed at the experienced (home-owning) gardener, who almost certainly had at least one gardener to command, if not several. Contributors included many of those who also fell into the category of the readers at which it was aimed, including several titled authors, and subjects ranged from 'Overhanging Trees' (a perennial of gardening periodicals) to 'Overcoming the Labour Problem' via 'Gladiolus', 'Cat Walks', 'Rock Gardening' and 'Gardening Overseas'. Advertisements addressed the need for tennis courts, revolving summerhouses, Lloyd Loom furniture and the advisability of writing a will. It was, in other words, just exactly the sort of periodical to welcome Beverley Nichols among its regular writers.

In January 1934 the first-ever edition of *My Garden* featured an article by Nichols entitled 'Given A Garden', where in typical 'exaggerated truth' he detailed the contents and original source of some of his own flowers.[12] In the 'League of Nations' border were plants which he had personally collected and smuggled in from other countries: the crocus from Switzerland, a rose geranium from Nice and a clump of heather from Mount Hymettus – along with a tortoise from the same location. The next garden area was the 'Thieves' Garden', and in this Nichols declared he grew solely 'stolen goods', which he had purloined as cuttings or roots from other gardens, an exercise which he declared to be extraordinary fun. Here were a cactus from the Jardin Exotique in Monte Carlo, gained at great personal risk from its poisonous spikes, and most importantly for our story, plum-coloured chrysanthemums from Kew Gardens.

Nichols described his theft of the plum-coloured chrysanthemums as being an act of 'utmost depravity'. A whole row of the chrysanthemums had greeted him in a Kew coolhouse one September, all replete with small cuttings 'like children clinging to their green skirts'. An attendant busy bending down to shift some pots had left them unprotected from his gaze, and Nichols 'darted out my hand, took the cutting and fled into the cold air, face crimson, heart thumping' and trembling so much in the act that he forgot to notice the label and thus had never known the name of this chrysanthemum. Recounting the daring tale, Nichols continued that he had promptly exited the gardens, noticing 'a huge noticeboard proclaiming dire penalties on all who dared to remove even a leaf or a twig from the sacred precincts'. Nichols hid the cutting in his 'hot overcoat pocket till I was safe on the other side of Hammersmith'. The chrysanthemum flourished exceedingly well and had provided Nichols with four large blooming plants, as well as the topic for an article, despite as he said having been 'rudely torn from the bosom of its rightful owners'.

It was perhaps this flagrant declaration of dishonesty, combined with the remark that his confessions probably rendered him liable to instant prosecution 'but I don't care', that rankled most with the authorities at Kew, to whom a review edition of this very first *My Garden* had almost undoubtedly been sent. A total of 50,000 copies of that first *My Garden* were printed, containing 50,000 declarations of the theft of the gorgeous plum-coloured chrysanthemums under the nose of one of their attendants, and the board of governors at Kew could not ignore it. The February edition of *My Garden* (1934) contained an innocent continuation of Nichols's musings on 'Given A Garden', but in March the editor was forced to print an apology on behalf of himself and also his 'whimsical' writer for the chrysanthemum thefts. Mr Beverley Nichols, he stated, had asked him to pass on his regret that some readers had very much resented some sentences in his January article relating to his 'Thieves' Garden'. Although intended as a piece of 'whimsical fooling' it had now come to their attention that theft from Kew and other public gardens was a 'serious menace', with prosecution for such acts resulting in penalties of up to £5.[13]

As if that wasn't bad enough, the Council of the Royal Horticultural Society had waded in with alarm on behalf of the growing band of private garden owners who generously opened their gardens under the new charitable garden scheme (started in 1927), worried that such thefts would encourage visitors intent on their own Thieves'

Gardens! The article, said the editor, had been intended as a joke, and had not condoned or encouraged the pilfering of plants after all, not even the most beauteous of plum-coloured chrysanthemums. Perhaps surprisingly, Beverley Nichols appeared again on the very next page with a third in the series of 'Given A Garden', this time on the subject of using only white flowers in a garden, with not a hint of plum chrysanthemums, and continued to be a regular contributor.[14] The name of the plum-coloured chrysanthemum which had caused all the trouble was never revealed.

The image of the chrysanthemum as an adjunct to any stylish upper-class decor such as that of Adela Pingsford is echoed in the description of the library of Lord Peter Wimsey, the aristocratic detective created by Dorothy L. Sayers. The library is described in the story *Whose Body?* (1923) as one of the most delightful bachelor rooms in London and appears to have combined elegance and academia with just a hint of the exotic:

> Its scheme was black and primrose; its walls were lined with rare editions, and its chairs and Chesterfield sofa suggested the embraces of the *houris*. In one corner stood a black baby grand, a wood fire leaped on a wide old-fashioned hearth, and the Sèvres vases on the chimneypiece were filled with ruddy and gold chrysanthemums.[15]

The visitor led into this vision from the raw November fogs of London recorded his impressions as being of something both 'rare and unattainable, but friendly and familiar, like a colourful and gilded paradise in a mediaeval painting'. Chrysanthemums, tawny on this occasion, were again present in the library alongside the rare editions in Sayers's *Clouds of Witness* (1926). Indeed the avid Wimsey reader might soon gain the impression that chrysanthemums are the only flower that Sayers and her famous detective were remotely interested in. As well as being present in the Wimsey library in *Clouds of Witness*, chrysanthemums appear in the death scene of the same novel, with the victim found lying amid boxes of bulbs and potted chrysanthemums in a small conservatory at Riddlesdale Lodge.

It comes as no surprise that when the bachelor Lord Wimsey eventually persuades the strong female lead character of Harriet Vane (herself a writer of detective fiction) to marry him, it is with chrysanthemums in her bouquet that she walks down the aisle. Their *Busman's Honeymoon* (1937) at the house of Talboys, where romance is interrupted by the advent of a dead body in the cellar, also includes the gathering of the 'bronze sheaves' of chrysanthemums from the garden and their display in the house, while the gardener (who will eventually be unmasked as the murderer) tends the autumnal flowers with a constancy he failed to find for his erstwhile elderly spinster admirer.

Written in the period between 1923 and 1937, the Lord Peter Wimsey stories are often mined for their representation of class and society in the inter-war period, and the constant presence of the

Chrysanthemums such as these could easily tempt a garden thief.

These cherry blossom and chrysanthemum lamps by E. Galle reflect
the fascination with the chrysanthemum in interior design in the
first decades of the 20th century.

chrysanthemums in shades of bronze and gold seem to shimmer
across the years as an evocation of bachelor libraries long since lost
to the world. The chrysanthemums cut down in their pride to make
way for vegetables in the Dig for Victory panic, as Britain entered
the Second World War in the autumn of 1939, literally mirror the
demise of the Wimsey library and way of life, although many a bride
went down the aisle with home grown 'mums' when little else was
left in the florists' shops.

The seeming ubiquity of the chrysanthemum in the respectable
(and less respectable) Victorian and Edwardian house led also to
poetic praises, and while Marianne North painted Japanese chrysanthemums her brother-in-law John Addington Symonds (1840–1893)
wrote poetry about them. In a paean of praise to both the flower and
the final months of the year that it presaged, Symonds pictured the

auroral hues of the chrysanthemum in rose, saffron and ivory, amber and amethyst:

> More delicate, more dear, more true than those
> Gay blossoms which the July sunbeams kissed,
> Purer of scent than honey heliotrope.[16]

Symonds was not perhaps as well acquainted with the bleak English November 'fretwork of frosts and winter frowns' as the poem might suggest, as by the 1870s he was spending much of his life abroad, in part due to his enthusiastic and public embrace of the cause of male homosexuality and in part due to a family predisposition to tuberculosis. In a typically Victorian attempt to suppress his homosexuality, Symonds had married Marianne North's sister Catherine in 1864. Despite the appearance of four daughters the marriage was not a success and his publication of a history of Greek *paiderastia* in 1873 led Marianne to describe the relationship as a disaster. Symonds and Catherine travelled together to Switzerland, in part for his health, and then parted company as he carried out a series of lecture tours and further publications on the same topic. During the last of these tours Symonds was accompanied by his lover, a Venetian gondolier named Angelo Fusato.

Most of Symonds's writings and verses were on the subject of Arcadian love in one form or another, and often contain coded references to what was at that period known as 'gross indecency'. However, in the case of this particular poem the fact that 'chrysanthemum' is also Japanese sexual slang for anus appears to be merely coincidence, and indeed was probably unknown to Symonds. Symonds recorded chrysanthemum flowers in his rooms at the family house in Davos, writing to a friend in October 1882 that 'Our rooms are filled now with roses and tuberoses from Cannes, violets and chrysanthemums from Sidbury,' Sidbury being the married home of his daughter Edith Harriet Symonds.[17] Katherine Mansfield admired Symonds and found 'a resemblance in myself' to him, suggesting more than a shared appreciation of the symbolism of chrysanthemums.[18]

In stark contrast to the Eastern tradition celebrating the nobility and beauty of the single flower in contemplative but uplifting philosophy, a feeling of decline and even decay dominates the chrysanthemum's appearance in English poetry: themes of autumn lingering before winter, a 'last stand' against decay and death as the inevitable frosts take their toll. Thomas Hardy (1840–1928) captures this in the 'Last Chrysanthemum', evoking the loneliness of a solitary flower that finally uncurls when all around 'leaves like corpses fall'. Published in 1901 in the volume *Poems of the Past and Present*, the verse was one of several in which Hardy questioned the wider pattern and relationship between God and nature and bears a close relation to Rudyard Kipling's later poem 'The Answer' (1922), with the questioning rose mourning the fate of a single broken bud, or Lawrence Binyon's 'The Burning of the Leaves', with its evocative 'last hollyhock's fallen tower'. An anonymous pre-1914 poem entitled 'Chrysanthemums' covers shades of rose and gold and amethyst in its first verse before continuing (with rather more similarity to Kipling's closely dated 'Glory of the Garden' than might be wise if wanting to avoid accusations of plagiarism):

> Oh, the glory of the garden, 'neath the clear pale Autumn sky,
> With the purple glow of pine-trees on the hill-slopes wild
>   and high.
> Oh the glint of tawny amber and the gleam of russet red,
> And the foam of white like snow-clouds, blown away from
>   realms o'erhead.[19]

John Betjeman (1906–1984), that most English of observers of the 1930s onwards, chose the image of the chrysanthemum to title his 1954 collection of poetry, *A Few Late Chrysanthemums*, of which a reviewer said 'It is rather as if something friendly, familiar and furry, easily frightened, had turned at bay and bitten one in the bathroom.'[20]

The
WINDOW
GARDEN
Series.

Série
FENÊTRE
sur le
JARDIN.

*Chrysanthemums
with Decorative Flower Pot.*

*Chrysanthèmes
avec Pot Artistique*

A postcard or a decoration?

Composed in the same late nineteenth- and early twentieth-century period as many of the literary appearances of the chrysanthemum was the elegy *Crisantemi* (Chrysanthemum), written by the composer Giacomo Puccini (1858–1924). Puccini was the heir apparent to Giuseppe Verdi in the world of Italian opera in the late nineteenth and early twentieth century, and with ten operas written between 1884 and 1924 (his last opera *Turandot* was unfinished at his death), he became the premier opera composer of his time. Puccini wrote very few instrumental works, but among them are four works for string quartet: three minuets and the elegy *Crisantemi*, written when Puccini was 32 years old. The elegy, supposedly written in a single night, was in memory of his friend the duke of Savoy, formerly King Amadeo I of Spain, who died in 1890. The title may be explained by the association in Italy between the white chrysanthemum and death and is occasionally rendered as *I Crisantemi* (The Chrysanthemum); this is a work of concentrated dark mood as the four instruments pay tribute to Puccini's friend. Puccini thought much of the two melodies used in the work as he reused them in the last act of his opera *Manon Lescaut* three years later, in 1893. The original version for string quartet is rarely heard as Puccini wrote a subsequent version for string orchestra which became more popular – if one can use this word for such a powerfully mournful piece.[21]

Amadeo I (1845–1890), king of Spain, whom the piece commemorates, was the second son of King Vittorio Emanuele II of Italy, but had a brief and fraught period as king in 1870–73, sandwiched between the death of Isabella II and the declaration of the First Spanish Republic. His life also included action in the Third Italian War of Independence, a period as vice-admiral of the Italian navy, marriage to the incredibly wealthy Donna Maria Vittoria and an assassination attempt, followed (understandably) by abdication. Returning to Italy, he was widowed and then married his French niece, Princess Maria Letizia Bonaparte, who was descended from Napoleon I. In all, a life worthy of a chrysanthemum or even an entire bouquet.

We will end our survey of chrysanthemums in literature (and music) with something rather more light-hearted. The name *Ju* (菊) (chrysanthemum) is a popular girls' name in China, and has begun to be used in its anglicized form by American Chinese families, despite the fact that its length makes it cumbersome and unusual in American society. The American writer and illustrator Kevin Henkes focused on this very theme in his 1991 children's story about a mouse named Chrysanthemum. The young mouse loves her long and exotic name until her first day at school, when she is teased about it by a girl named Victoria and her friends Rita and Jo, with their tiny names. Comforted by a music teacher with the rather wonderful name of Mrs Delphinium Twinkle, as well as by her own parents, young Chrysanthemum learns to love her name again, and when Mrs Twinkle gives birth to a daughter at the end of the book, she calls her Chrysanthemum too.

This story gives a wonderful word-image of the term chrysanthemum as 'beautiful', 'and precious and priceless and fascinating and winsome' – and indeed everything that both the young Chrysanthemum and the flower she is named after are. With its delightful illustrations and its easy-to-assimilate story of overcoming 'differences' which are so easily magnified by other children into cruel teasing, the book was turned into an animated story narrated by Meryl Streep. Perennially popular, it was voted as one of the 'Top One Hundred Picture Books' in a 2012 poll by the *School Library Journal* (coming in at number 66) and also one of the 'Teachers' Top Ten Books for Children' in America. Its popularity has also given rise to an increasing number of children of differing nationalities being named Chrysanthemum.[22]

seven

Meaningful and Useful:
A Plethora of Chrysanthemums

❧

As the artist William Morris famously said, 'Have nothing in your houses that you do not know to be useful or believe to be beautiful', to which one might reasonably add 'or which you do not feel to be meaningful'.[1] The chrysanthemum has been recognized by ancient and modern Eastern and Western cultures for its beauty, but now we must turn to its meaning and utility.

In Eastern cultures, the chrysanthemum was imbued and embedded with cultural and religious symbolism, but its delayed arrival in the West did not deter those who were anxious to assign a meaning to it in the more light-hearted Western 'language of flowers'. Floriography, as it is more correctly known, was introduced into England, or in actual fact reintroduced, in the early eighteenth century, supposedly by Lady Mary Wortley Montagu (1689–1762). While the meaning of flowers had a long history in Europe, most especially in the medieval and Tudor periods, these were often religiously inclined and had little in common with the complex 'language' that was soon to become fashionable at all levels of society thanks to Lady Mary.

Lady Mary had discovered, more properly rediscovered, floriography in the harems of the Ottoman court in Turkey, where it was used to communicate with erstwhile admirers under the ever-vigilant eyes and ears of the harem guards. The flower-language craze lasted longest in England, where it was at its height between around 1820 and 1870, equating with much of the Victorian era when morals

Gartenflora 1892. Taf. 1373.

CHRYSANTHEMUM INDICUM. A LOUIS BOEHMER. B. H. BALLANTINE
Verlag von PAUL PAREY in Berlin.
Chromolith. Gustav Leutzsch, Gera, Reuss.

Despite its perfection in all other ways, the colour of the chrysanthemum might make it unwelcome in a bouquet. 'Chrysanthemum indicum', from E. von Regel, *Gartenflora*, vol. XLI (1892).

Who would send a postcard depicting the yellow chrysanthemum of jealousy and slighted love?

were increasingly restrictive and direct communication between the sexes controlled in an echo of the way in which the sexes were separated in Turkey. In France it lasted a somewhat briefer period between around 1810 and 1850, and in the United States just for twenty years from 1830 to 1850, whether due to more fickle fashions or less prescriptive social rules, who can say?

As with many new fashions, the uninitiated turned to books and periodicals for instruction on how to correctly apply the new rules of posies, bouquets and corsage decoration. In America, the language of flowers attracted the attention of one of the most popular women writers and editors of the day, Sarah Josepha Hale (1788–1879). Hale was the long-time editor of the *Ladies' Magazine* and co-editor of *Godey's Lady's Book*, as well as the authoress of the children's poem 'Mary Had a Little Lamb'. In 1832 she brought out *Flora's Interpreter*, which was to become the best-selling work on the language of flowers in America, and which continued to be edited, enlarged and revised into the 1860s.

Some of the earliest British floral dictionaries were rather surprisingly by men, including Henry Phillips's *Floral Emblems*, published in 1825, and Frederic Shoberl's *The Language of Flowers; with Illustrative*

Poetry (1834), but perhaps the most popular and long-lasting was the relatively late entrant to the genre, Kate Greenaway's *Language of Flowers*, first published in 1884 and still in print today as much for its illustrations as its meanings. Although not all of the guides to floral language agreed with each other (surely a distinct disadvantage if trying to carry on a passionate affair or conduct complex negotiations regarding the exact status of one's relationship commitment?), postcards of the late nineteenth century generally settled on a colour division for the meaning attributed to chrysanthemums, as was also the case for carnations, tulips and roses.

This simplification along colour lines was convenient for those who found the difference between incurved and reflexed difficult to grasp, or indeed difficult to obtain from a florist. Red chrysanthemums were a brave statement of 'I love' (presumably the recipient was the subject of the love), the yellow chrysanthemum 'slighted love' or jealousy, while the white chrysanthemum, associated with death in other countries, completed the all-too-brief journey from love to jealousy by adding the message of 'undisguised and often bitter truth'. At which point it seemed only right to turn to the traditional Chinese

A bright future awaits the recipient of this birthday card, 1908.

symbolism of the chrysanthemum as representing 'cheerfulness in adversity'. If there was any hope of conciliation at all in this whirlwind romance played out in flowers, then an ox-eye daisy counselling 'patience' might be called upon, or that other denizen of the autumn flower border, the Michaelmas daisy, which betokened 'afterthought'.[2] Dramatic though this tale in chrysanthemums might be it did not rival the message of the dried white rose, which single-handedly betokened 'death preferable to loss of innocence'. By having several meanings dependent on colours the chrysanthemum had more language capabilities than many other flowers of longer standing in the West, although the rose was the most loquacious, with 33 meanings if you included rosebuds and the thornless rose.

In its native China and Japan the chrysanthemum already had meanings somewhat less transitory perhaps than the West's brief flirtation with floral languages. Unlike other white flowers, the white chrysanthemum is not associated with death and ghosts in China, but instead represents nobility and elegance from being favoured by the Chinese poet Tao Qian. Due to their long flower life and use in some herbal medicines and teas, the chrysanthemum in China was generally, and is still, associated with a strong life force. Because of this they are traditionally a favoured gift to the elderly. The health and condition of the bloom is also far more important in China than in the West, where to receive flowers at all is often considered sufficient and to query their exact petal arrangement would seem both pedantic and ungrateful. However, in China the quest for the perfect harmonious petal configuration is part of paying attention to the gift and an ideal chrysanthemum could be mistaken for a carved netsuke figure.

Unlike the Chinese, who see the association of chrysanthemum with old age as a positive life force, much of mainland Europe is rather more pessimistic over the prospects confronting the autumn of life. In France, Italy and Spain, the autumnal chrysanthemum is a flower of endings rather than new beginnings, of death rather than life. In the Catholic calendar, All Saints' Day, in honour of all saints and

White Chrysanthemum
Sincerity

WHAT sweeter flowers
Could I send you,
For these mean truth,
And I am true.

Sincerity or death — depending on which country you are in, white chrysanthemums have very different meanings.

martyrs, falls on the first of November, followed by All Souls' Day (Day of the Dead) on the second. The days, and often several days before and after, are marked by visitors to cemeteries carrying bunches, pots and even entire wheelbarrows full of the autumnal flowers as the living commemorate the dead and the two come closest together at the changing of the season. Florists work overtime to ensure the pots of chrysanthemum arrive at the right grave in the vast urban cemeteries. On All Saints Day, known as Toussaint in France (literally 'All Saints'), chrysanthemum sellers take over the pavements outside the cemeteries, brightening dull autumn days with yards of pavement covered in a full spectrum of colour.

In Italy, the chrysanthemum is a flower so intimately associated with death and the funereal that to give one in a bouquet or as a pot plant is to invite death in. An advertisement for a British bank boasting of its cultural awareness played on just this symbolism in 2017. An English man living in Italy brings chrysanthemums to a woman who has had an accident on her moped: in England a natural enough gift to someone who has been ill or for some reason needs cheering up. Not wanting to disturb her he leaves the flowers on her doorstep. However, in Italy passers-by see the battered moped and the flowers on the doorstep and assume the woman has died. Neighbours weep for her and the street goes into mourning. When the woman steps outside the next day, the old ladies in the street think they are seeing a ghost and hurriedly cross themselves to ward off evil, a misunderstanding in cultural symbolism.

Despite being an autumn/fall flower in the Western Hemisphere, the chrysanthemum is in bloom in May for much of the Southern Hemisphere, making it an excellent choice for Mother's Day bouquets in Australia, while in America the chrysanthemum corsage was worn by mothers attending their son's first soccer match in the autumn term or the first parental visits of that season to the college student freshly away from home. A recent American blog on chrysanthemums even calls the chrysanthemum 'soccer mums' from this association. In both instances the connection between mothers and chrysanthemums has made it a traditional flower gift, with any Victorian connotations of love, jealousy and despair long forgotten or disregarded.

Having explored the European meanings that have been attributed to the exotic chrysanthemum, we must turn finally to the more mundane usages to which this 'golden flower' has been put, for which we need to track back again both to its original arrival and its close relatives, some of which were already in Europe and others of which arrived with it from the East.

When the chrysanthemum arrived in England in the late eighteenth century there was some debate as to exactly what plant it was. Some claimed that it was actually related to the chamomile (*Anthemis tinctoria*), while others declared it was unmistakably a feverfew or even a tansy, but it was generally settled that, despite the first ones introduced actually being a deep red, it should still be called a chrysanthemum.[3]

The name is, of course, not the original Chinese term. That was considered by the scientists of Europe to be impossible to incorporate into the established classifications of the period – not to mention hard for them to pronounce and impossible to write. In fact there was already a flower called the chrysanthemum in Europe before the 'real' chrysanthemum set foot there, and that was the sunflower, which had been named *Chrysanthemum Peruvianum* by herbalists and botanists of the sixteenth century. First depicted in 1583 by the Dutch botanist Rembert Dodoens in his *Stirpium historiae*, the plant proudly bore its new name on the depiction, itself having been rechristened from its Native American name. By 1597, when it appeared in John Gerard's *The Herball; or, Generall Historie of Plantes*, published in London, the sunflower had become the Indian Sun, or Great Marigold of Peru, or in botanical Latin: *Flos Solis major*, or *Corona Solis*, or *Sol Indianus* (one sees a sun motif emerging here) and the term *Chrysanthemum Peruvianum* was only glancingly referred to as a name given by 'others'. The Latin

Chrysanthemum ornamentation at Montmartre Cemetery, Paris.

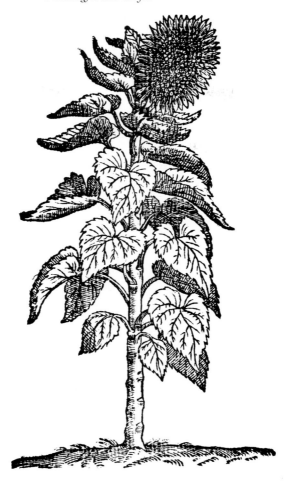

term for the sunflower is now *Helianthus*, which literally means 'sun flower', but in Greek rather than Latin, and it has long since ceased being confused with a chrysanthemum.

In 1629 John Parkinson, one of the founding members of the Worshipful Society of Apothecaries and an excellent botanist and herbalist, indexed three different 'chrysanthemums' in his *Paradisi in Sole Paradisus Terrestris*: *Chrysanthemum odoratum*, *Chrysanthemum Peruvianum* and *Chrysanthemum Creticum*. The *Chrysanthemum Peruvianum* we have already met; the *Chrysanthemum Creticum* was the 'Corne Marigold of

Although technically *Helianthus* (the sun flower), the sunflower appears to have as much claim to the description 'chyrsos'.

Candy': a 'fair corne marigold' with a single stalk over half a metre (2 ft) high and a pale yellow flower 'rising out of a scaly head' and composed of ten to twelve petals, distinct in its habit from 'other corn marigolds'.[4] Seekers of the *Chrysanthemum odoratum* in the index to Parkinson's work were referred to its alternative name of *Chamemelum nudum*, or the 'naked' chamomile; although because checking on this index entry merely referred you on yet again to 'Camomilla and C. vulgaris', which finally told you to look on page 290, where you would find the long-sought Chamomile which had also previously been classified as a chrysanthemum. Although by then you might have decided that the plant was too confusing to bother with. The common flower which until recently we might have recognized as a chrysanthemum relative, the ox-eye daisy, was instead referred to as *Buphthalmem vulgare*, now of course *Leucanthemum vulgare* but until recently in the chrysanthemum genus. Isn't historical botany a wonderful thing?

The 'other' corn marigold which Parkinson referred to was the *Chrysanthemum segetum* now known as *Glebionis segetum* (although still botanically noted as 'syn.' or 'synonym' as its botanical ousting from being a chrysanthemum only occurred in 1999). The leaves are deeply lobed and the 'relationship' with chrysanthemum can be easily seen even if nowadays not officially recognized as such. Originally native only to the eastern Mediterranean, this eventually spread to western and northern Europe and, rather ironically, into China, where it is used as a vegetable. Unlike the more decorative and aristocratic chrysanthemum, however, the corn marigold or corn daisy has never been a welcome guest for gardeners or farmers. In the thirteenth century, a law of Alexander II of Scotland (1198–1249) stated that any farmer who allowed so much as a single plant of corn marigold to produce seed among the crops would be fined a sheep. This does seem rather harsh for what is basically a rather attractive tall yellow daisy with petals often touched by white at the edges, but it is an invasive weed.

In 1523 the corn marigold was in trouble again, being noted in Sir Anthony Fitzherbert's *Boke of Husbandrie* as being 'an yll wede, and groweth commonlye in barleye and pees', although it could be used in the garden as a decorative flower.[5] It was also noted as a serious pest of fields in the Victorian period, but as with so many once-common arable weeds has declined to the point of almost rarity with the common use of herbicides and modern seed-cleaning techniques. Wildlife bodies note its useful attractiveness to bees and butterflies and in particular to the rather alarmingly named chamomile shark moth, and its seeds can now be bought to enhance wildflower mixes on light and acid soils. However, with up to 13,500 seeds on any individual plant one wouldn't have thought you needed to ever buy more than a starter pack.[6]

Leucanthemum orientale Tournef. Chrisanthemum bipinnatum Lin. Sp. Pl. 1255.
Ital. Piletro, Erba cipressina. Gall. La grande Marguerite orientale.

This wonderful late 18th-century image encapsulates the confusion of the chrysanthemum. None of the names appended to it exist in modern taxonomy.

Another plant which has at times been awarded the 'chrysanthemum' title is the daisy-like feverfew. Easy to grow, it is native to Eurasia, originating in the Balkans, but long ago spread to northern Europe. Feverfew has a small, bright, daisy-like flower with white petals and a sunny yellow centre. It loves to grow in sunny places and spreads rapidly by seed to overwhelm flowerbeds on dry slopes. The feverfew was originally classified by herbalists of the seventeenth and eighteenth centuries as *Chrysanthemum parthenium* but later became *Pyrethrum parthenium*, before being finally (one hopes) transferred yet again to become *Tanacetum parthenium*, aligning itself with the tansy, which was also once a chrysanthemum.

Originally given the common name 'featherfew' after its feathery leaves, the feverfew is widely regarded as most useful for fever, arthritis and headaches and is recorded as being used as an anti-inflammatory in the first century AD. It may well have been introduced into England from central Europe by the Romans, who used it for these medicinal properties, as evidenced by its inclusion in the works of the Greek/Roman physician Dioscorides. In his 1597 *The Herball; or, Generall Historie of Plantes* John Gerard did not hazard a guess as to the feverfew's familial or (in modern terminology) genetic associations, but instead listed its virtues in physic, including being a remedy for 'those of a melancholic nature' who might be 'sad, pensive or without speech'.[7] Grieve's *Modern Herbal* recommends planting Corn Feverfew around the dwelling house to purify the atmosphere and allay distressing sensitivity to pain and other emotions, or more practically for wound healing and blood clotting.[8] Feverfew has attracted renewed interest in its medicinal usage thanks to its parthenolide content, which preliminary research indicates may have an impact on cancer-cell growth.

It was traditionally known as 'bachelor's buttons', a naming it shared with cornflowers. Explanations for the derivations of this vary from the flower literally having the appearance of a button, to the wearing of a small posy of such flowers in the buttonhole to indicate romantic availability. The *parthenium* part of the plant's name, which has remained constant, contains a reference to virginity, but this meaning (or the Latin name) is unlikely to have been known to the country folk who originated the name 'bachelor's buttons' or the alternative 'pale maids'.

Lining motorway embankments and newly disturbed ground, the most commonly seen chrysanthemum in northern Europe today is the wild and often invasive *Chrysanthemum leucanthemum* or ox-eye daisy. A perennial grassland wildflower, it has spread as far afield as North America, New Zealand and Australia, as well as through the heartlands of Europe and the temperate regions of Asia. Its modern success, some would call it over-success, is due to its method of re-generation combined with its bitter taste. Propagating by rhizome as well as seed, small plants quickly multiply even from fragments of the rhizome so that grass-cutting machinery results in multiplication rather than eradication. Although the unopened flower buds can be marinated and used as a substitute for capers (how desperate can one be for a caper?), Grieve's *A Modern Herbal* records that 'the taste of the dried herb is bitter and tingling, and the odour faintly resembles that of valerian.'[9]

Tanacetum parthenium: once the featherfew, now the feverfew.

Cattle will not eat it, and even rabbits only give it a passing nibble when the young leaves first appear, and so it multiplies in grazing meadows where there are no longer farm labourers employed to remove thistles and dock and other such weeds, including the daisy.

However, although environmentalists may despair of the ox-eye, particularly in countries where it is non-native, many a driver is grateful for the spectacular sheets of white daisies that cover motorway embankments through the late spring and early summer months. Unlike the poppy, the seeds only remain viable for two to three years, and so although it leaps in on newly grass-seeded areas it cannot out-compete where hand pulling is employed. A garden invaded by the bright white 'moon daisy' can be rectified, if wished, by a determined weeding of the distinctive rosettes in the summer and autumn. Its alternative common name of 'moon daisy' refers to its white face rather than any association with the waxing or waning of the moon, and the alternative 'dog daisy' merely refers to its commonness (as with 'dog rose' and 'dog violet'). The name ox-eye (or bull's-eye) is more difficult to understand as few healthy cattle have white and yellow eyes.

In herbal medicine the ox-eye daisy is used as an anti-spasmodic, a diuretic, as a cure for night sweats and a nerve tonic. It is perhaps because of this combination that it was long associated with 'women's medicines' and given its alternative common names 'maudlin daisy' or 'maudlin wort' (the latter by Gerard), a corruption of St Mary Magdalene. It was also used as a decoction added to ale for jaundice and other hepatic diseases, although this may have been linked to the 'doctrine of signatures' which dictated the use of a yellowing plant to cure a disease that resulted in a yellow skin. Another alternative common name, 'butter daisy', also reflects the intense yellowness of the large centre of the flower. The scientific name by which it has been officially known for centuries, *Chrysanthemum leucanthemum* (which literally meant 'gold flower white flower'), has now been changed and it has been reclassified as *Leucanthemum vulgares* (or 'common white flower') as part of the general shake-up of the aster or daisy family

The common marguerite or ox-eye has medicinal usages which have resulted in its being recorded in early herbals such as this by the French botanist Jean Baptiste François Pierre Bulliard (c. 1742–1793).

and the ousting from the chrysanthemum fold of anything other than the decorative florists' or hardy garden chrysanthemum.

The juggling of the chrysanthemums has its roots rather literally in a reassessment of the genus itself, which in 1999 was welcomed back from its time in the wilderness of the genus *Dendranthema*. This renaming of the genera has been contentious, but a ruling of the International Botanical Congress in that year changed the defining species of the genus to *Chrysanthemum indicum*, restoring the florists' chrysanthemums to the genus *Chrysanthemum* and ousting others into the genera *Glebionis*, *Argyranthemum*, *Leucanthemopsis*, *Leucanthemum*, *Rhodanthemum* and *Tanacetum*.

Also shaken out of the fold was the traditional herb 'costmary', once upon a time *Chrysanthemum balsamita*, occasionally *Balsamita vulgaris*, sometimes *Chrysanthemum tanacetum*, and now a combination of the two as *Tanacetum balsamita*, but with no hint of a chrysanthemum. Regardless of this modern glitch it deserves a mention in any history of the chrysanthemum as it was also once known as *Chrysanthemum grandiflorum*, although why that should be is a mystery given that its flowers are tiny bud- or button-like things, the only 'grand' thing about them being that they grow in clusters. As with most wild plants there are some

Roadsides of ox-eye daisies have become a common and heart-lifting sight in northern Europe.

doubts as to its origins. Its name associates it with Mary or St Mary and in herbal medicines it was widely used for 'women's diseases', which from the medieval period up to the late nineteenth century could include anything from hysteria to menstruation, urinary issues to 'softening the hardness of the mother'.[10]

In the seventeenth century the herbalist Nicholas Culpeper recorded that the plant was 'under the dominion of Jupiter' and in addition to softening mothers would

> gently purgeth choler and phlegm, extenuating that which is gross, and cutting that which is tough and glutinous, cleanseth that which is foul, and prevents putrefaction; it openeth obstructions and relieves their bad effects, and it is beneficial in all sorts of dry agues. It is astringent to the stomach, and strengtheneth the livers and other viscera: and taken in whey, worketh more effectively. Taken fasting in the morning, it relieves chronic pains in the head, and to stay, dry up, and consume all their rheums or distillations from the head into the stomach, much to digest raw humours gathered therein. It is profitable for those that are fallen into a continual evil disposition of the body, called cachexy, especially in beginning of the disease. It is good for weak and cold livers. The seed is given to children for worms, and so is the infusion of flowers in white wine, about two ounces at a time. It maketh an excellent salve to heal old ulcers, being boiled with oil of olive, and adder's tongue with it; and after is strained, put in a little wax, rosin and turpentine to make it as thick as required.[11]

Given this all-round beneficial action it was just as well that it grew easily in the garden and had a distinctive, easily recognizable scent of mint and balsam combined, giving it the alternative name of mint geranium. It was also known as alecost and used in beer when hops were not available, giving an equally distinctive flavour. What is less understandable is its common use as a page marker in bibles: perhaps the scent repelled silverfish or booklice or mice, although another suggestion is that sniffing the strong herb might keep you alert during long sermons – rather wonderfully described in a 2008 book by Jack Staub (*75 Exceptional Herbs For Your Garden*), where he envisages 'snoozy Christians avoid[ing] incipient coma by inhaling the stirring scent'.[12]

Likely to cause a rather more permanent coma is the chemical pyrethrum contained in many of the chrysanthemum family. Although most chrysanthemums are admired for their exquisite petals, magnificent heads, autumnal hues or just for plain being there when all else is dead or dying, the *Chrysanthemum cinerariifolium* has long been praised by gardeners in need of a deadly potion. *C. cinerariifolium* – and its close companion *Chrysanthemum coccineum* – contain a cocktail of chemicals including pyrethrins, cinerolones and chrysanthemines, which together form powerful contact insecticides. Pyrethrum in powdered or liquid form was one of the most commonly used aphid killers in the Victorian garden and remained a popular insecticide into the late twentieth century. In order to obtain the chemical, the flowers and seed heads were traditionally soaked in water or you could buy a ready-made powder created from the extract of the seed heads or as an oleoresin.

The powder or oleoresin could be floated in water or oil, or used straight in the case of the powder, and blown or sprayed onto the plants and their surroundings. The pyrethrin attacks the central nervous system of the insect, killing it, and in the case of malaria-carrying mosquitoes, stopping it biting. In Victorian gardens the powders and sprays were used with gay abandon and handled with little or no precautions, with garden boys as young as eleven or twelve sent into glasshouses to spray the chemical around in dense mists. Under modern health and safety legislation there is a recommended exposure limit (REL) of 5 mg/m^3 over an eight-hour workday, which would have been meaningless to Victorian gardening boys, who worked from dawn to dusk. People exposed to pyrethrum may experience symptoms including pruritus (itching), dermatitis, papules, erythema (red skin), rhinorrhea (runny nose), sneezing and asthma. At levels of 5,000 mg/m³, pyrethrum is immediately dangerous to life and health.

In fact pyrethrin is less toxic to mammals and birds than many other synthetic insecticides and is also relatively quick to biodegrade in the environment, although it is harmful to fish. This ability to biodegrade, plus its origin as a natural product, means that it is extensively used in organic agriculture and horticulture – such that it has become an important economic product. Modern production is based in Tasmania, although traditional producers were centred in Kenya (which produced 6,000 tonnes of the world's pyrethrum in 1998) and Ecuador. If you are cautious about spraying anything at all on your fruit and vegetables you may like to just plant some (pyrethrum) chrysanthemums in among your other produce as the mere presence is thought to discourage aphids, spider mites, leafhoppers and cabbage worms, as well as being used to shoo away bedbugs.

There are other species that also contain pyrethrin, notably *Chrysanthemum balsamita* (the tansy) and *Chrysanthemum marshalli*, but both have much smaller concentrations than the *cinerariifolium*. In fact the *Chrysanthemum cinerariifolium* and the *Chrysanthemum coccineum* have now been reclassified as *Tanacetum* (*T. cinerariifolium* and *T. coccineum*), which would be marginally less confusing if the whole of what had once been the genus *Pyrethrum* had not also been, leaving no pyrethrums at all, although the term is still used to refer to the active agent of the insecticide. So, just to be clear – the chrysanthemums that produce pyrethrin, some of which were historically classified as 'pyrethrums', have all now been reclassified as tanacetums, although the chemical they are grown for is still named pyrethrin.

For those of us with a less than scientific bent it may be easier to bypass the whole classification debate and continue using the 'common' names for these delightfully deadly plants: the Dalmatian chrysanthemum (*C. cinerariifolium*) and the Persian chrysanthemum (*C. coccineum*) as well as the Dalmatian insect flower, Persian insect flower, Dalmatian pellitory and Persian pellitory. It was probably the

C. coccineum that was the source of anti-lice powder which originated in the Middle East and was commonly known as Persian Powder or Persian Pellitory. In the modern period this was trademarked by the Austrian industrialist Johann Zacherl and sold worldwide under the brand Zacherlin lice powder, although it will also kill bedbugs. Tip: go to bed with a chrysanthemum!

Pellitory is another of those plant names that can lead one in a merry dance as the common name is used for a variety of plants including the *Anacyclus pyrethrum* (Spanish pellitory and Mount Atlas daisy), *Achillea ptarmica* (European pellitory, sneezewort yarrow or white tansy), *Parietaria officinalis* (Pellitory-of-the-wall) and so on. Of these only the *Anacyclus pyrethrum* (Spanish pellitory) would seem to have any relation to the Persian or Dalmatian pellitory – until one learns that in fact it does not contain any pyrethrum! However, both the *Anacyclus pyrethrum* and the *Achillea ptarmica* share with the chrysanthemums and tanacetums a family connection, being all recognizably from the daisy or Asteraceae family. The Dalmatian chrysanthemum is a clear white-petalled daisy-like flower with a sunny yellow centre, while *C. coccineum*, as its name would suggest, is also available in vivid reds and pinks but has no relation to the food colouring cochineal, which ironically comes from insects.

The *Chrysanthemum coronarium*, or garland chrysanthemum, has been discovered to have properties of its own as an anti-fungal. The active substance is again in the seeds as a protein with mitogenic (cell dividing) activity. The *coronarium* was actually cultivated in Britain by 1629 and is now an annual of waste places and roadsides, as well as invading arable fields. It is native to the Mediterranean and East Asia and is one of the few annual chrysanthemums. It is also one of the few that are considered not only edible but highly nutritious and is a traditional addition to vegetable dishes in Asia (where it is known as Chop Suey Greens, *Kikuna* or *Shingiku*). In Turkey, the young plants are sliced and fried with garlic and flour before being boiled. Recent research has suggested that the properties of *C. coronarium* may extend beyond being anti-microbial to anti-tumour properties, but this claim is at an early stage. If this is the case it seems rather a shame for chrysanthemums as a whole that *C. coronarium* has been reclassified as *Glebionis coronaria*. Seeds can still be purchased, however, under the name of *C. coronarium*, including the cultivar 'Primrose Gem'.

Although traditional herbalism is less popular in Europe today than it was in the seventeenth century, in Chinese medicines the chrysanthemum is still widely used as a tisane to treat influenzas and a range of other infections, while the cooling effect is also supposed to help with fevers, inflammations and heatstroke. A rinse made from the flowers or a cream is used for skin infections, while it is also drunk as an aid to digestion. High blood pressure or hypertension can also be treated by chrysanthemum according to traditional Chinese medicine.

In Korea chrysanthemum tea is used as a 'pick me up' and there are a variety of ways to take it. The basic tea is made from dried flowers collected before opening. The flowers are blanched in bamboo salt water, carefully washed in cold water and drained on kitchen towel and then covered with *hanji* (handmade paper) and dried in an *ondol* (floor-heated) room. When served, three to four flowers are added to hot water. The rather sweeter honey chrysanthemum tea is created by preserving the flowers in honey for three to four weeks before using while a specialized Korean medicinal tea is created by a more complex washing and drying procedure. Flowers are washed carefully, then steamed using water mixed with a herbal decoction and dried. When fully dried, they are steamed again, and dried again. This process is repeated nine times. Water to decoction ratio can be 8:1, and the decoction includes dried roots of white woodland peony, steamed and dried roots of rehmannia, dried roots of Korean angelica and dried roots of lovage; although the main ingredient is the chrysanthemum flower steamed in the mix.

In China there are several varieties of chrysanthemum used to make tea, very much in the same way that there are different tea plants. The colour of the tea ranges from white to pale or bright yellow according to the flower-head used. Packs of loose tea with flower-heads are commonly available, as are pre-packaged chrysanthemum tea-bags as well as cartons of a ready-made drink similar to an iced or cool drink, often heavily sweetened. Since it is safe to drink for most people and may calm the nerves and have added anti-bacterial properties there seems no reason not to try it — especially as (other than as the sweetened ready-made drink) it contains zero calories. Official advice suggests that you ask your doctor before embarking on a medicinal course of chrysanthemum tea.

Also supposedly health-giving is the 'chrysanthemum stone' or 'flower stone' found most often in the Hunan and Hubei provinces of China, although also as far afield as Korea and even the western USA. The stone is usually a grey or sometimes brown limestone, found most often in riverbeds, and containing within it a radiating white mineral that, after being exposed on a flat plane by slicing and polishing, appears to radiate out from a centre like a burst of flower petals and bears a striking resemblance to a petrified chrysanthemum.

Chrysanthemum stones are considered lucky. This one originated at Daxi River, Liu Yang, Hunan, China.

Bons
baisers

63/1

NÉO · PHOT
· PARIS ·

'Good embraces' is the translation of this French postcard from the 1920s.

Miyagawa Hanzan,
baluster vase
with stylized
chrysanthemums,
c. 1895.

The actual flowers are usually composed of the minerals celestite or calcite, radiating from a small chert centre. These stones range in size from 5–8 centimetres to 50 centimetres in diameter (2–3 in. to almost 20 in.), and the more flower-like the pattern the more expensive the stone.

Like the chrysanthemum, the chrysanthemum stone is said to help in times of transformation: forging through obstacles to bring joy, love and abundance in your life, it helps you reach your true potential and can be held in the hand while you are clarifying your goals or looking for the next step on your path. Traded for thousands of years, these stones were until recently only obtainable through East–West trading routes along with rare silks and teas, but nowadays this help-mate to transforming your life can be obtained online, often in suspiciously repetitive and regular patterns. To help Westerners appreciate the beauty and culture of the chrysanthemum stone there is now a guide by the authors Thomas Elias and Hiromi Nakaoji containing more than 120 images of some of the best and rarest petalled stones. The authors also tell you how to identify a fake stone, although, unlike all the other chrysanthemums discussed in this book, even the most splendid of the chrysanthemum stones sadly contain no real chrysanthemum.

When the winter chrysanthemums go,
there's nothing to write about
but radishes.
Matsuo Bashō (松尾 芭蕉, 1644–1694)

Growing in the Hill Close, Warwick, collection of hardy chrysanthemums, this exquisite bloom defies the English weather to bring exoticism from the East.

Timeline

c. 1600–1046 BC	First cultivation of the chrysanthemum recorded in Shang Dynasty China
AD 618–907	Numerous types of chrysanthemum being grown in Tang Dynasty China, their differing petals and hues celebrated in Chinese literature
910	First record of an imperial chrysanthemum show in Japan
Mid-1400s	First Chinese text on chrysanthemums; four hundred cultivars in a range of colours recorded by this time
1583	The *Chrysanthemum Peruvianum* is depicted in Rembert Dodoens's *Stirpium historiae*
1736	The first Xiaolan Chrysanthemum Show takes place
1795	*Chrysanthemum indicum* first arrives at London's Colville Nursery
1796	*Chrysanthemum indicum* is described and pictured in William Curtis's *Botanical Magazine*
1846	Robert Fortune introduces the Chusan daisy or 'Pompom' chrysanthemum to England
1858	Samuel Broome publishes *Culture of the Chrysanthemum, as Practised in the Temple Gardens* and popularizes the chrysanthemum with a series of shows at London's Inner Temple Garden

1876	Emperor Meiji, the 122nd emperor of Japan (1867–1912), creates the Supreme Order of the Chrysanthemum
1884	Founding of the *National Chrysanthemum Society* (UK)
1908	Publication of *The Flowers and Gardens of Japan* by Florence and Ella Du Cane
1910	'Japan-British Exhibition' is held in London, popularizing all things 'Oriental', including the chrysanthemum
1937	Publication of John Steinbeck's 'The Chrysanthemums' in *Harper's Magazine*
1938–	Development of the *Chrysanthemum* x *rubellum* by the nurseryman Amos Perry from an original 'sport'
1947	Founding of Cambridge and District Chrysanthemum Society
2000 onwards	Collection and establishment of National Collection of Chrysanthemums (UK) by Judy Barker at London Colney, St Albans
2016	Expansion of National Collection of Chrysanthemums (UK) to be a dispersed collection at Hill Close, Warwick, and Norwell Nurseries in Nottinghamshire as well as London Colney

References

Introduction

1 John Salter, *The Chrysanthemum: Its History and Culture* (London, 1865), p. 3.

1 The Honourable and Imperial Flower

1 Noel Kingsbury, *Garden Flora: The Natural and Cultural History of the Plants in Your Garden* (Portland, OR, 2016).
2 Ibid.
3 'Legends of the Chrysanthemum', *My Garden*, I/I (1934), pp. 54–6.
4 Basil William Robinson, *Kuniyoshi* (London, 1961).
5 Gian Carlo Calza, *Hokusai* (London and New York, 2003), p. 7.
6 *Popular Science Monthly*, VI (February 1890), pp. 531–5.
7 Kingsbury, *Garden Flora*, pp. 82–7.
8 Ian Ruxton, ed., *A Diplomat in Japan: The Diaries of Ernest Satow, 1870–1883*, annotated and indexed by Ian Ruxton (Morrisville, NC, 2009), p. 459.
9 Ibid., p. 25.
10 Ibid.
11 Marguerite James, 'Chrysanthemums in the East', *My Garden*, I/I (1934), pp. 71–5.
12 Arthur Herrington, *The Chrysanthemum: Its Culture for Professional Growers and Amateurs. A practical Treatise on its Propagation, Cultivation, Training, Raising for Exhibition and Market, Hybridising, Origin and History* (New York, 1905), p. 155.
13 Ibid., pp. 155–6.
14 'Legends of the Chrysanthemum', pp. 54–6.
15 Ruth Benedict, *The Chrysanthemum and the Sword: Patterns of Japanese Culture* (Boston, MA, 1946), p. 2.

2 Smuggling Tea and Chrysanthemums

1 Jakob Breyne, *Prodromus fasciculi rariorum plantarum secundus*, available at https://bibdigital.rjb.csic.es, accessed 2 September 2019.

195

2 Judith Taylor, *An Abundance of Flowers: More Great Flower Breeders of the Past* (Athens, OH, 2018).

3 Arthur Herrington, *The Chrysanthemum: Its Culture for Professional Growers and Amateurs* (1905), p. 151.

4 Henry Phillips, *Flora Historica; or, The Three Seasons of the British Parterre* (London, 1824), pp. 397–411.

5 Allen Paterson, 'Philip Miller: A Portrait', *Garden History*, XIV/1 (1986), pp. 40–49. Hazel Le Rougetel, 'Miller, Philip (1691–1771)', *Oxford Dictionary of National Biography*, Oxford University Press, 2004, www.oxforddnb.com, accessed 17 August 2017.

6 Arthur Herrington, *The Chrysanthemum: Its Culture for Professional Growers and Amateurs. A Practical Treatise on Its Propagation, Cultivation, Training, Raising for Exhibition and Market, Hybridising, Origin and History* (New York, 1905).

7 Margaret Willes, *The Gardens of the British Working Class* (New Haven, CT, 2014).

8 William Curtis, *The Botanical Magazine; or, Flower-garden Displayed*, IX (February 1796), pp. 326–30.

9 Joseph Sabine, 'Observations on the Chrysanthemum Indicum of Linnaeus read by Joseph Sabine', *Transactions of the Linnean Society*, XIII (18 December 1821), pp. 561–80.

10 Taylor, *An Abundance of Flowers*.

11 Herrington, *The Chrysanthemum*, p. 151.

12 Phillips, *Flora Historica*, pp. 397–411.

13 Ibid., p. 400.

14 Ibid.

15 Emil Bretschneider, *History of European Botanical Discoveries in China* (1898), pp. 211–13. Bretschneider states that Sir Abraham Hume was a fellow of the Horticultural Society. He had a garden at his estate Wormleybury in Hertfordshire, where he cultivated many rare exotic plants. (Trans. Hort. Soc. IV, 59.)

16 Quoted in Alice M. Coates, *Flowers and Their Histories*, 2nd edn (1968), p. 52.

17 Herrington, *The Chrysanthemum*, p. 150.

18 Mure Dickie, 'A Tale of Tea Grown in the Scottish Highlands', *Financial Times*, 1 January 2016, www.ft.com.

19 *The Gardeners' Chronicle* (18 December 1841), *advertisements* (no page no.).

20 *The Gardener's Magazine*, XI (1868). Quoted in John Salter (1798–1874) and the origin of (Variegated) Species Part 1 and Part 2: On Website 'Tall Tales From The Trees', talltalesfromthetrees.blogspot.com.

21 *The Gardeners' Chronicle and Agricultural Gazette* (29 April 1865), p. 390.

22 Ibid.

23 Ibid.

24 John Salter, *The Chrysanthemum: Its History and Culture* (London, 1865).

25 Herrington, *The Chrysanthemum*, p. 154.

26 *New International Encyclopaedia* (New York, 1902).

3 Gathering the Harvest in Societies and Shows

1 Ruth Duthie, *Florists' Flowers and Societies* (Aylesbury, 1968).
2 *Floricultural Cabinet*, vol. 1 (March 1833), p. 3, referenced in Margaret Willes, *The Gardens of the British Working Classes* (New Haven, CT, 2014), p. 109.
3 H. Haworth, 'A New Arrangement of the Double-flowered Chinese Chrysanthemums, with An Improved Method of Cultivation', *Gardener's Magazine and Register of Rural & Domestic Improvement*, IX/43 (April 1933), p. 222.
4 Ibid., p. 225.
5 Judith Taylor, *An Abundance of Flowers: More Great Flower Breeders of the Past* (Athens, OH, 2018).
6 F. W. Burbidge, *The Chrysanthemum: Its History, Culture, Classification and Nomenclature* (London, 1884), p. 106.
7 Quoted by Simon Brown, Past Master of the Garden of the Inner Temple, in Samuel Broome, *The floral oracle of the working classes*, author's ms copy.
8 Willes, *The Gardens of the British Working Classes*, p. 225.
9 Ibid., p. 247.
10 Ibid., p. 246.
11 *New International Encyclopaedia* (New York, 1902).
12 Quoted by Simon Brown, Past Master of the Garden of the Inner Temple in Broome, *The floral oracle*; also *The Inner Temple Year Book, 2014–15* (London), pp. 54–7.
13 Ibid.
14 Ibid.
15 Ibid.
16 Ibid.
17 *Gardeners' Chronicle* (29 January 1870), pp. 146–7.
18 Quoted by Simon Brown, Past Master of the Garden of the Inner Temple in Broome, *The floral oracle*; also *The Inner Temple Year Book, 2014–15* (London), pp. 54–7.
19 The section on the Inner Temple and Samuel Broome is courtesy of Simon Brown, Past Master of the Garden of the Inner Temple.
20 I am grateful to the garden writer Anna Pavord for the information that the use of beer bottles for showing is still alive and well in the Wakefield and North of England Tulip Society.
21 See 'History of the National Chrysanthemum Society', www.nationalchrysanthemumsociety.co.uk, accessed 22 August 2017.

4 In Peace and in War

1 Judy Barker, *Hardy Garden Chrysanthemums* (Evesham, 2018), p. 12.
2 Ibid., p. 10.
3 *Gardeners' Chronicle*, vol. XX (17 November 1883), p. 633.

4 *Gardeners' Chronicle* (13 December 1913), p. 413.

5 See 'Chinese Porcelain', www.rothschildarchive.org, accessed 7 July 2019.

6 Margaret Willes, *The Gardens of the British Working Classes* (New Haven, CT, 2014).

7 Stephen Cheveley, *A Garden Goes to War* (London, 1940), p. 18.

8 Ibid., p. 18 (both quotes).

9 Arthur Herrington, *The Chrysanthemum: Its Culture for Professional Growers and Amateurs. A Practical Treatise on Its Propagation, Cultivation, Training, Raising for Exhibition and Market, Hybridising, Origin and History* (New York, 1905), p. 156.

10 Ibid.

11 Peter Henderson, *Practical Floriculture* (Chicago, IL, 1892 edn), p. 237.

12 Herrington, *The Chrysanthemum*.

13 *Chicago Tribune*, 17 July 1891, p. 8.

14 See 'Longwoods Garden Chrysanthemum Festival', https://longwoodgardens.org, accessed 19 October 2017.

5 An Impression of Chrysanthemums

1 Ann Dumas, 'Monet's Garden at Giverny', in *Painting the Modern Garden: Monet to Matisse*, ed. Clare Willsdon et al. (London, 2015), p. 54.

2 See https://fondation-monet.com/en/claude-monet/quotations, accessed 7 May 2019.

3 Jane R. Becker, 'Caillebotte's *Chrysanthemums*, or, Unexpected Encounters with Impressionist Interior Design', 12 August 2015, www.metmuseum.org.

4 Ian Chivers, ed., *Oxford Dictionary of Art and Artists*, 4th edn (Oxford, 2009), p. 628.

5 BBC online Gardening Guide to Plants/Plantfinder: Entry for Shasta daisies, www.bbc.co.uk/gardening, accessed 6 May 2019.

6 See 'Dennis Miller Bunker, *Chrysanthemums*, 1888', www.gardnermuseum.org, accessed 10 October 2018.

7 Ibid.

8 Quote from Mondrian in his letter to Theo van Doesburg, 1915; as cited in the 'Stijl' catalogue (1951), p. 71; quoted in H.L.C. Jaffé and J. M. Meulenhoff, *De Stijl, 1917–1931: The Dutch Contribution to Modern Art* (Amsterdam, 1956), p. 6.

9 Jane Neet, 'Mondrian's "Chrysanthemum"', *Bulletin of the Cleveland Museum of Art*, vol. LXXIV/7 (September 1987), pp. 282–303.

10 Quote from Mondrian about 1905–10, in Piet Mondrian, *Essays* ('Plastic Art and Pure Plastic Art', 1937 and his Other Essays (1941–1943) (New York, 1945), p. 10; as cited in Jaffé and Meulenhoff, *De Stijl 1917–1931*, p. 40.

11 Neet, 'Mondrian's "Chrysanthemum"', pp. 282–303.

12 Judith Taylor, *An Abundance of Flowers: More Great Flower Breeders of the Past* (Athens, OH, 2018).

13 The Gardens Trust Blog (anon.), 'Two Essex Girls and The Exotic: Ella and Florence Du Cane', https://thegardenstrust.blog, 11 November 2017.

14 Ella and Florence Du Cane, *The Flowers and Gardens of Japan* (London, 1908), p. vii.

15 Ibid., p. 200.

16 Ibid., p. 201.

17 Ibid., pp. 201–2.

18 Ibid.

19 Ibid., pp. 204–6.

20 Alison Redfoot, *Victorian Watercolorist Ella Mary Du Cane: A Study in Resistance and Compliance of Gender Stereotypes, the Professional Art World, Orientalism, and the Interpretation of Japanese Gardens for British Society* (Long Beach, CA, 2011). See also the Gardens Trust Blog (anon.), 'Two Essex Girls and The Exotic'.

21 *Country Life*, 14 March 1925, pp. 388–41.

22 John Claudius Loudon, *The Gardener's Magazine and Register of Rural and Domestic Improvement*, vol. VII (1831), p. 95.

23 Royal Botanic Gardens Kew, *A Vision of Eden: The Life and Work of Marianne North* (New York, 1980), p. 235.

6 A Literary Bouquet

1 Originally printed in *Harper's Magazine* (October 1937), pp. 513–19: this is now most easily accessed as an online text at www.literaryfictions.com.

2 Charles Sweet Jr, 'Ms Elisa Allen and Steinbeck's "The Chrysanthemums"', *Modern Fiction Studies*, 20 (1974), pp. 210–14.

3 John Steinbeck, 'The Chrysanthemums', *Harper's Magazine*, 1049 (October 1937).

4 Katherine Mansfield, 'The Singing Lesson', in *The Garden Party* [1920] (London, 2007).

5 'The Singing Lesson' (1920), available on the website of the Katherine Mansfield Society, www.katherinemansfieldsociety.org (unpaginated text), accessed 7 July 2019.

6 *English Review*, vol. VIII (June 1911), pp. 415–33.

7 Ibid., p. 421.

8 Ford Madox Ford, *Portraits from Life* (Boston, MA, 1937).

9 Joseph Cowley, *The Chrysanthemum Garden* [1981] (Lincoln, NE, 2000).

10 Saki, 'The Stalled Ox', in *The Penguin Complete Saki* (London, 1976), pp. 345.

11 Ibid.

12 Beverley Nichols, 'Given A Garden', *My Garden* (January 1934), pp. 19–26.

13 'An Apology' by the editor, *My Garden* (March 1934), p. 335.

14 Beverley Nichols, 'Given A Garden: White in the Garden', *My Garden* (March 1934), pp. 336–42.

15 Dorothy L. Sayers, *Whose Body?* (1923), available at https://digital.library.upenn.edu.

16 John Addington Symonds, 'To Chrysanthemums', in *The Garden Anthology*, selected and arranged by Irene Osgood and Horace Wyndham (London, 1914), p. 14.

17 Horatio Brown, *John Addington Symond: A Biography Compiled from his Papers and Correspondance* (London and New York, 1908), p. 378.

18 Andrew Eastham, *Aesthetic Afterlives: Irony, Literary Modernity and the Ends of Beauty* (London, 2011).

19 Anon., 'Chrysanthemums' (n.d.), in *The Garden Anthology*, p. 15.

20 Quoted by Raymond Carr in 'The Teddy Bares His Teeth', *The Spectator*, 26 September 2007.

21 Alan Beggerow, 'Puccini – I Crisantemi (Chrysanthemums)', muswrite.blogspot.co.uk, 31 January 2017.

22 Kevin Henkes, *Chrysanthemum* (New York, 1991).

7 Meaningful and Useful: A Plethora of Chrysanthemums

1 'The Beauty of Life', a lecture before the Birmingham Society of Arts and School of Design (19 February 1880), later published in *Hopes and Fears for Art: Five Lectures Delivered in Birmingham, London, and Nottingham, 1878–1881* (London, 1882).

2 Kate Greenaway, *Language of Flowers* (London, 1884).

3 Arthur Herrington, *The Chrysanthemum: Its Culture for Professional Growers and Amateurs. A Practical Treatise on Its Propagation, Cultivation, Training, Raising for Exhibition and Market, Hybridising, Origin and History* (New York, 1905).

4 John Parkinson, *Paradisi in sole, paradisus terrestris* [1629] (London, 1904), p. 295.

5 Plantlife, 'Corn Marigold', www.plantlife.org.uk, accessed 8 May 2019.

6 Henry Doubleday Research Association figures.

7 *Gerard's Herbal*, ed. Marcus Woodward (London, 1985), p. 151.

8 Maude Grieve and Mrs C. Leyel, *A Modern Herbal* (Mineola, NY, 1972), vol. I, p. 310.

9 Ibid., p. 288.

10 Grieve and Leyel, *A Modern Herbal*, p. 260.

11 *Culpeper's Complete Herbal* [1653] (Ware, Hertfordshire, 1995), p. 78.

12 Jack Staub, *75 Exceptional Herbs For Your Garden* (Salt Lake City, UT, 2008), p. 55.

Further Reading

Barker, Judy, *Hardy Garden Chrysanthemums* (Evesham, 2018)

Benedict, Ruth, *The Chrysanthemum and the Sword: Patterns of Japanese Culture*, rev. edn (Rutland, VT, 2018)

Du Cane, Florence, and Ella, *The Flowers and Gardens of Japan* (London, 1908)

Herrington, Arthur, *The Chrysanthemum: Its Culture for Professional Growers and Amateurs. A Practical Treatise on Its Propagation, Cultivation, Training, Raising for Exhibition and Market, Hybridising, Origin and History* (New York, 1905)

Musgrave, Toby, Will Musgrave and Chris Gardner, *The Plant Hunters: Two Hundred Years of Adventure and Discovery around the World* (London, 1998)

Sabine, Joseph, 'Observations on the Chrysanthemum Indicum of Linnaeus read by Joseph Sabine', *Transactions of the Linnean Society*, vol. XIII (December 1821), pp. 561–80

Salter, John, *The Chrysanthemum: Its History and Culture* (London, 1865)

Taylor, Judith, *An Abundance of Flowers: More Great Flower Breeders of the Past* (Athens, OH, 2018)

Watt, Alistair, *Robert Fortune: A Plant Hunter in the Orient* (London, 2016)

Wilkinson, Anne, *The Victorian Gardener* (Stroud, 2006)

Willsdon, Clare A. P., et al., *Painting the Modern Garden: Monet to Matisse* (London, 2015)

Associations and Websites

GARDEN CHRYSANTHEMUMS
www.gardenchrysanthemums.org.uk
Run by Judy Barker, who holds the National Collection of Hardy (garden)
Chrysanthemums on allotments in Hertfordshire and the national collection
at Hill Close, Warwick. These are mainly varieties dating to the 1920s–70s.

HARDY PLANT SOCIETY
www.hardy-plant.org.uk
Formed in 1957, an international society which provides members with
information on familiar and less well-known perennials, including the
hardy garden chrysanthemum. They have published a handbook on hardy
chrysanthemums, written by Judy Barker (2018).

NATIONAL CHRYSANTHEMUM SOCIETY (UK)
www.nationalchrysanthemumsociety.co.uk
This website offers a lot of information on the exhibition type of
chrysanthemums in the UK, with a link to the garden types.

NATIONAL CHRYSANTHEMUM SOCIETY (USA)
www.mums.org
A very active website which includes the sale of T-shirts with the slogan
'mum's the word', reflecting the term most often used for chrysanthemums
in America.

POINT GREY CHRYSANTHEMUM ASSOCIATION
www.chrysanthemumsvancouver.com
Members of the Point Grey Chrysanthemum Association are dedicated
to keeping mums blooming through shows, talks and also special events
including sales.

CHRYSANTHEMUMS IN ABERDEEN
www.chrysanthemums.info
Website maintained by breeder and exhibitor Paul Barlow, based in
Aberdeen but covering shows and breeds across Scotland and the north.
The Aberdeen Chrysanthemum and Dahlia Society was formed in 1956.

HUMBERSIDE CHRYSANTHEMUM CLUB
www.bevlee.karoo.net
Set up around 1980, this is one of the largest UK show clubs, with annual
shows in Preston in September and November.

WOOLMANS PLANT NURSERY
(specializing in chrysanthemums)
www.woolmans.com
Growers of chrysanthemums for 130 years and partnered with the National
Chrysanthemum Society (UK).

CAMBRIDGE MUSEUM, NEW ZEALAND
http://cambridgemuseum.org.nz/chrysanthemum-society
The website for this museum contains fascinating information on the history
of chrysanthemum growing in New Zealand from 1891 onwards and news of
the modern Waikato Flower Societies.

Acknowledgements

I would like to thank Simon Brown (Past Master of the Inner Temple Garden) for sharing the material on Samuel Broome, head gardener of the Inner Temple, and also for providing images of the chrysanthemum tiles in the building that was until recently Lloyds Bank, and which commemorated the link between the Inner Temple and the chrysanthemum. Also Celia Pilkington, the archivist for the Inner Temple. Lucy Paquette, novelist and specialist on the artist James Tissot, was generous with information on the model in the painter's work *Chrysanthemums*. Colin Salter, descendant of John Salter, generously allowed quotations from his website, www.talltalesfromthetrees.blogspot.co.uk. Patrick Miles of the Cambridge and District Chrysanthemum Society provided fascinating discussions and also kindly asked me to speak to the society, where I was able to meet other devotees. Alex Forest, chief curator of the Grand Rapids Public Museum, Michigan, generously helped to track down the painting by Mathias Alten. Terry Brignall, of Glatton, traced and shared the image of Beverley Nichols and his partner Cyril Butcher at their house in Glatton. Judith Taylor's superb book on *An Abundance of Flowers: More Great Flower Breeders of the Past* came out during the final edit of this book (2018) and was responsible for some of the facts and figures regarding the modern market in chrysanthemums and the histories of individual breeders who have nurtured the chrysanthemum. Finally I would like to thank Michael Leaman for his patience and understanding when this book was delayed.

Photo Acknowledgements

The author and publishers wish to express their thanks to the below sources of illustrative material and/or permission to reproduce it:

Alamy: pp. 8 (Granger Historical Picture Archive), 11, 179 (Florilegius), 46 (The Protected Art Archive), 189 (Heritage Image Partnership Ltd); akg Images: pp. 117, 128 (De Agostini Picture Library), 140 (Antoine Pascal), 159 (Sotheby's), 172 (Gerard Degeorge); author's collection: pp. 10, 13, 30, 40, 41, 54, 79, 88, 105, 132, 133, 137, 138, 142, 167, 168, 169, 188, 191; Biodiversity Heritage Library: pp. 51, 52, 55, 104, 131; Boston Public Library: p. 91; botanicalillustrations.org: pp. 15, 69, 101, 147, 166; British Library, London: p. 87; Courtesy of Simon Brown: p. 86; Flickr: pp. 6, 23, 94 (F. D. Richards), 9 (Tdlucs5000), 16–17 (Joe de Sousa), 25, 38 (Marufish), 28 (Hsing Wei), 58 (Verity Cridland), 62–3 (Carmin.shot), 70 (Chimpmunk_1), 78 (Shou-Hui Wang), 112, 158 (Kathryn), 143 (Liz West), 178 (Andrey Zharkikh), 181 (Diego Charlón Sánchez); Isabella Stewart Gardner Museum, Boston: p. 124; Parent Géry: p. 187; Getty Images: p. 68; Eric Glass Ltd and Delaware University: p. 154 (British Combine Photos Ltd. With thanks to Terry Brignall); Reproduced courtesy of the Grand Rapids Public Museum, MI: p. 125; Stephen Kemp: p. 114; Library of Congress, Washington, DC: p. 43; The Metropolitan Museum of Art, New York: pp. 12 (H. O. Havemeyer Collection, Bequest of Mrs H. O. Havemeyer, 1929), 20 (The Harry G. C. Packard Collection of Asian Art, Gift of Harry G. C. Packard and Purchase, Rogers, Harris Brisbane Dick and Louis V. Bell Funds, Joseph Pulitzer Bequest, and the Annenberg Fund Inc. Gift, 1975), 29 (Fletcher Fund , 1929), 33 (Gift of Estate of Samuel Isham, 1914 (JP1016), 34 (H. O. Havemeyer Collection, Bequest of Mrs H. O. Havemeyer, 1929), 42 (Gift of Lincoln Kirstein, 1959), 97 (Gift of Mrs Richard E. Linburn, 1978), 118 (Gift of the Honorable John C. Whitehead, 2014); Museum of Fine Arts, Boston: pp. 32 (William Sturgis Bigelow Collection. Accession Number: 11.36489a-b), 37 (William Sturgis Bigelow Collection. Accession Number: 11.22027), 162 (Leonard A. Lauder Postard Collection – Gift of Leonard A. Lauder. Accession number: 2014.5415); National Archives and Records Administration (NARA), Washington, DC: p. 110; NHM Images: p. 59.

Index

Page numbers in *italics* refer to illustrations

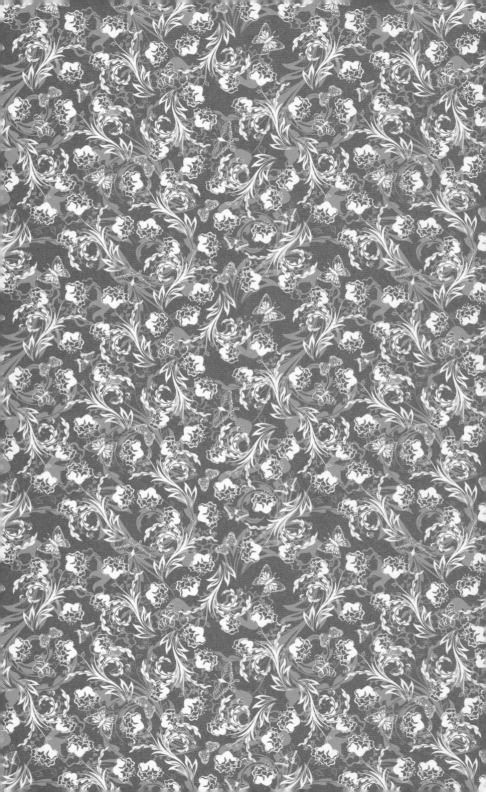